THE HANDBOOK OF OFF-ROAD DRIVING

2nd EDITION
(REVISED AND ENLARGED)

JULIAN CREMONA AND KEITH HART

Ashford, Buchan & Enright
Leatherhead

Published by Ashford, Buchan & Enright, 31 Bridge Street, Leatherhead, Surrey KT22 8BN

Text © Julian Cremona and Keith Hart 1993
Photographs © Julian Cremona except where otherwise indicated

Whilst great care has been taken in the compilation of this book, neither author nor publisher can accept responsibility for the use, or consequences of the use, of the information and opinions expressed herein; nor for any inaccuracies or mishaps arising from the work.

British Library Cataloguing in Publication Data

Cremona, Julian
  The handbook of off-road driving.
  1. Great Britain. Rallycross
  1. Title II. Hart, Keith
  796.7′2

ISBN 1 85253 285 8

Typeset by Priory Publications, Haywards Heath
Printed by FotoDirect Ltd, Brighton, Sussex

Contents

Preface

Driving off road is fun. It can also be dangerous and damaging, both to you and the terrain over which you pass. Our purpose in writing this book is to explain how to drive off road in a safe and responsible way, minimising damage to both environment and vehicle. Our book is for anyone interested in off roading: a novice can use it to learn the ropes but we hope that even an expert will be able to glean some new ideas. Between the two of us there are forty years of off-road experience (although Keith has the edge!) Much of this knowledge came from making mistakes and, hopefully, we can help you not to make so many.

The subject of off roading is vast but we have tried at least to touch on its many facets. This includes explaining some of the 'foreign language' that has grown up around the subject. We concentrate on the variety of techniques that you are likely to need: for example, climbing, traversing and going down hills. We try to give you the confidence needed to attempt the crossing of mud, sand and wading deep water. Then, when you become well and truly stuck we deal with recovery techniques in Chapter 5!

Eventually, all off roaders will follow their own different avenues as their experience grows. For you, perhaps, just pottering down a green lane may be what off roading is all about; others may want to know how to tow heavy loads such as horseboxes. Others yet, may want to feel the adrenalin surging through their veins and will take up an off-road motor sport such as trialling or racing against the clock. Ultimately, there is travel and the expedition. This can be the most demanding off-road experience, but there is no reason why anyone with a 4x4 should not involve themselves in this. In our penultimate chapter we cover most aspects of expedition preparation not only of the vehicle but also, and just as important, yourself. Finally, we make a few suggestions about where you can off road abroad.

It is, of course, impossible to really learn everything from a book - you just have to get out there and do it for yourself. So, go get those tyres muddy!

Acknowledgements

Off roading has a very social and gregarious nature. Over the years we have found that fellow enthusiasts have always been pleased to share experiences and pass on knowledge. David Bowyer has been of considerable help especially in supplying winching and other equipment for us to photograph. This we were able to do at his off-road driving school in Devon. Thanks must also go to the staff of Brooklyn Engineering near Southampton for their assistance, over the years, in Land Rover preparation and spares. They also supplied tyres and towing equipment for the illustrations in this book.

Many of the photographs used in the techniques section were taken on locations organised by Mike Wooley, Tavistock Tree Services, and Simon Allen of A & H Rallying (South West). Although our own 4x4s were used as the main models we would like to thank Rob Carter, Geoff Cooper, David and Catherine Garrad for help in the past. David Shephard has a tremendous knowledge of off roading and it is typical of him to share this knowledge with others. It was his idea to include in the book a section on bush winching.

Dr Exton Arnold has helped by discussing with us various technical matters including security systems. Ray Bevin has given us advice and technical information on Kinetic Energy Recovery Rope (KERR) technique including the recovery formula. Dr John Elliot has always given us assistance on expedition medical matters and he helped to compile the list of typical ailments and their treatment. Thanks must go to the many students of St Mary's College, Southampton who, over the past fifteen years, have been involved in the yearly college expedition - for some it was just a beginning before going on to mount their own overland expeditions. Others who have helped, like Pieter and Ida Kersten, we have met whilst on expedition.

Our thanks must go, too, to Robert Chote, friend and colleague on a number of expeditions. He has read the manuscript and made a number of criticisms and helpful comments, all of which we have carefully noted. However, any mistakes are purely our own. We also thank Matthew and Mary Hart for the use of their 'half-way house' in Dorset, the ideal meeting place between our homes, to discuss the manuscript. The meal service was excellent!

Finally, had it not been for the help, support and encouragement given by our wives, Brenda Cremona and Val Hart, the publication of this book would have been impossible.

Julian Cremona   *Keith Hart*
Southampton, Hants   *North Tawton, Devon*

September, 1993

The author and publisher would like to thank David Roffey for the use of his Range Rover for the cover picture. Cover picture by Julian Cremona.

Introduction
to Off Roading

Remember, above all else, that all land belongs to someone. You cannot just take to the hills! The presence of a dirt track or even the impression of tyre tracks on grass does not mean there is access.

In the United Kingdom most of the areas open to drivers are shown on the Landranger Ordnance Survey maps (but note that the status of these areas is constantly changing). These public rights of way are commonly termed 'green lanes'. Their true definition is a 'Byway Open to All Traffic'; BOAT for short, or a Road Used as a Public Path (RUPP). The pink markings used in an Ordnance Survey map 1:50,000 series is +-+-+- for a BOAT or ._._._ for a RUPP. If you intend to drive green lanes you must first check the definitive map. These byways are controlled by the local County Council. Under existing law, the council must keep the byways open and must also keep a definitive map showing access to them. A visit to the council offices with your Ordnance Survey map can easily verify such access. If a byway is found to be obstructed, e.g. by a farmer's gate, the council should be notified immediately.

Green laning can be great fun and the feeling of remoteness, away from Tarmac roads, is exhilarating. However, carried out irresponsibly, green laning can create considerable difficulty for the responsible majority. In recent years bad publicity has been attracted to off roading and green laning by careless individuals whose activities have left much to be desired. An experienced and truly professional off roader will leave a byway as he or she found it; that is, without damaging vegetation or deepening ruts. Tread lightly!

Most byways are ancient roads that have been established for hundreds of years, e.g. the Ox Drove that crosses Wiltshire and Hampshire. Routes such as this one are signposted and clearly shown on maps. They cross beautiful stretches of countryside and even in the middle of summer few people will be seen on them. Some, like the Ridgeway in Berkshire, are becoming over-used and

Fig. 1.1 *Waiting for a tow out of the mire – a Hamlet cigar moment; always green lane in pairs. (Courtesy of Justyn Willsmore)*

are best avoided on Sundays and Bank Holidays at the height of the season. At these times hiking and horse riding are also at their peak. Many groups of people use these lanes and it is important for all concerned that we 'get along'. You must exert self-discipline and follow the golden rules:

- never go green laning solo: if you become stuck another vehicle can usually pull you out creating a minimum of fuss
- never go out in large groups of vehicles – four at most – as damage/disturbance is intensified
- do not drive too fast – 20 mph maximum
- always shut gates after passing through
- always be polite when meeting farmers/landowners and other users – you will be driving over someone's land and the only right you have is to pass through
- slow right down, even stop, when meeting other users
- ensure that holes are filled in and removed material is replaced (if debogging a stuck vehicle requires digging or the moving of logs/vegetation from the side of the byway)

Please ensure a minimum of disturbance at all times. Have concern for the environment.

1

Vehicles:
Exploding the Myths

IN THE BEGINNING

In the last few years the number of four-wheel drive (FWD) vehicles has snowballed. Once upon a time schoolboys dreamt of fast cars. Now the emphasis is split; for many it is the off-road vehicle that appeals. The off-road boom has arrived!

The year 1993 saw the 45th anniversary of the Land Rover, which was a design developed from the American Willys jeep. It was the gathering war clouds of 1939 which stimulated the design of the jeep, a lightweight military reconnaissance vehicle. Although FWD vehicles had been produced earlier this century, it was not until the 1940s that they were mass produced. Thousands arrived in the United Kingdom, shipped from United States production plants during the Second World War, and afterwards many remained and continued life in agriculture. By 1948 Maurice Wilks of the Rover Company had instigated the Land Rover based on the pattern of the jeep. Forty-five years and four major revisions later it has an extensive cult following, which has been supplemented by the success of twenty-four years of Range Rovers.

For many years Toyota have tried to rival these 4x4 vehicles with their own Land Cruisers; the fourth production model arrived in Great Britain in 1992 and is winning great acclaim. Nissan brought in its first competitor, the Patrol, in 1983. During the 1970s Suzuki developed a cheap off-road van for the Third World but its success was greater in the West where there was an existing niche for a small off roader. The van gave birth to the SJ series which sold more than a million worldwide. Every major car manufacturer has or is now developing a FWD vehicle, some specialising in off-road capability.

Japanese vehicles are generally flashier, have brighter paintwork and their design pays great attention to detail in the provision of, for

Fig. 1.2   Where it all started – a restored Willys Jeep being used in trialling

example, the dashboard gauges, tilt meters and upholstery. They also have an excellent record for reliability. The steel bodies of these vehicles do eventually lead to rusting, whereas the aluminium panelling of the Land Rover helps in maintaining a considerable longevity. However, until recently the Land Rover's rather spartan interior and lack of comfort has tilted the market somewhat in favour of the Japanese vehicles. Since 1990 the battle has been raging with the huge success of the Discovery Land Rover. The Range Rover maintains the prestige at the top with the introduction of the LSE model in late 1992. We are due for a major UK assault, sometime in the mid-1990s, with the all-new Range Rover.

In recent years FWD vehicles have been arriving in the United Kingdom from Eastern European countries. For example, the Lada Niva is a low-cost vehicle that has had a large following throughout Europe since 1978; another, even cheaper, alternative is the Dacia Duster series which has been produced for several years, although it has had a somewhat chequered history in the UK. Though very basic and rather old fashioned these vehicles are inexpensive and good value for money, but do tend to depreciate rapidly.

German and Austrian vehicles are very well made and comfortable. The snag is that they are very expensive and tend to be spartan inside considering the prices. Spares are also very expensive.

WHY FWD?

So you want, or you already have, a FWD vehicle. Why and what for? Let us look at the various reasons.

The leisure and general market
Many people buy a FWD car, especially the smaller models from Suzuki and Daihatsu, because of the different image that it creates – robustness and adaptability immediately spring to mind. This part of the market is huge. Few of these owners realise or understand the full potential of their vehicle.

Business
Farmers, builders, developers, construction engineers, surveyors etc. have demanded off-road vehicles for many years. Forestry departments and the water, electricity and gas boards increasingly require sophisticated off-road vehicles. Many Land Rovers have been developed with these groups specifically in mind.

Towing
Many off-road vehicles are bought by people wanting to tow caravans, boats and horseboxes. This is not just for the possibility of driving off Tarmac but because of the low-range gearing available.

Expeditions
In the Royal Geographical Society's Expedition Yearbooks for 1983 to 1985, well over 1,000 major expeditions originating from the United Kingdom were listed, and many more left without being recorded. Some 80 per cent required the use of vehicles with off-road capability. Chapter 9 of this book deals specifically with expedition work.

PROCEED WITH CAUTION

Perhaps you bought a vehicle for one of the above reasons or alternatively just for some off-road fun. Whatever the reason remember that 4x4 vehicles are not only costly to buy but also to run. Many people buy them because of the slower depreciation value and the fact that, being a more robust form of transport, they carry on when most two-wheel-drive vehicles are reaching the end of their lives. It is only after buying the 4x4 of their dreams that many people discover the high cost of running it. Preparation before and brief maintenance after off roading is therefore essential to keep costs to a minimum. (This is dealt with in more detail in Chapters 3 and 6.)

Your choice of vehicle may be a difficult one. Try not to go bigger than you really need. The extra weight and size could cost you dearly in fuel bills. But, at the same time, do not try to tow two hunters in a horsebox behind a Suzuki. It is also a fact of life that most off roaders do not fit in modern garages! If this is important to you it could be a little disappointment that leads to early disenchantment.

Before you go out and buy all the latest off-road accessories, especially those for recovery, we suggest that you watch other people on off-road trials or, better still, take a course at a good off-road school (see Useful Addresses). Courses are great fun for both novice and expert and different types of recovery equipment will be displayed and demonstrated by the instructors. This is the time to make up your mind about what extra gear to purchase. It is also the best way to learn techniques such as winching.

There are four basic pieces of equipment essential for self recovery: a high lift jack; a strong shovel; a length of suitable rope, and a pair of heavy-duty gloves. Each of these will be dealt with in some detail in Chapter 5.

Off-road schools and a wide variety of accessory dealers advertise in magazines like *Off Road & 4 wheel drive*, *International Off-Roader* and *Land Rover Owner*. The All-Wheel Drive Club (AWDC) which began in 1968 and attracts membership even from those without a vehicle, can provide a series of useful publications and advice and also organises field meetings. In addition, there are several specific clubs which cater for the off roader, and most have rights-of-way officers. If you are interested in green laning you should join one, as they will have survey forms that can be filled in to keep everyone up to date on green lane routes. (See Useful Addresses.)

THE JARGON – WHAT DOES IT ALL MEAN?

As with any specialist subject matter, terms grow and develop within it. Enthusiasts take this still further, creating 'in' words that few outsiders really understand. However, this need not be so complicated; communication of terms is important and in this section we hope to dispel any mystery over the main jargon used within off-road circles. (See also the Glossary.)

The transmission system
It is the transmission system of the off-road vehicle that makes it so distinct from others and gives it its versatility.

Many 4x4 vehicles employ live axles (Fig. 1.3); this, of course, means a vehicle capable of driving all four wheels at the same time (instead of the normal two) to give better traction and power. A normal two-wheel drive vehicle has just one prop shaft coming from the gearbox. So that four wheels can be driven a second prop shaft emerges to connect with the other pair of wheels. The gearbox must therefore be larger than usual to accommodate the extra prop and

Fig. 1.3 General transmission layout of 4x4 vehicles with live axles. Solid arrows represent power flow when in two-wheel drive. Outline arrows represent components turned by front wheels, with subsequent loss of energy (acn be avoided if freewheeling hubs are fitted)

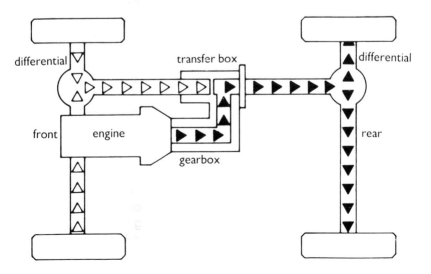

differential   transfer box   differential

front   engine   rear

gearbox

be able to transfer power to the second set of wheels. To this end it has a dedicated region called the transfer box. This box of tricks is like a second gearbox since, for most vehicles, it has two sets of gear ratios known as high- or low-range gears. A lever on the transfer box will allow selection of either range of gears. Top speed of the low range of ratios, in fourth gear, will reach around 25-35 mph. Its merits lie in the pulling and climbing power that can be achieved by such low ratios. Conversely, this power can be used for exceptional engine braking when descending steep slopes. With care, low range can be transferred to high range whilst moving. When in low range virtually any gear can be used to pull away because of the low ratios present. Upon selecting low range gears the vehicle will automatically be in FWD.

The 4x4 vehicle will be either part-time or full-time FWD. In the full-time case the driver has no option as the drive is fixed. On part-time vehicles there will be a knob or lever connecting through to the transfer box which switches the drive from just the rear two wheels, in order to put all four wheels into operation.

Fig. 1.4 Power flow of permanent 4x4 in slippery conditions, without centre diff. locked

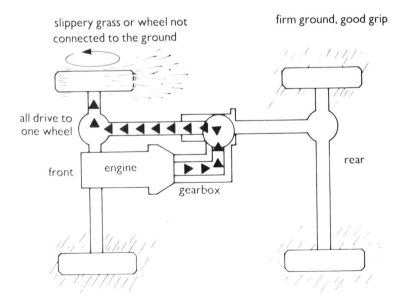

Use two-wheel drive whilst driving on paved roads as all-wheel drive should only be engaged on rough terrain. The reason behind this is what is termed transmission *wind-up*. Remember, when FWD is engaged all the wheels are being forced to turn at the same time and revolution. Driving dead straight on a dry, firm surface will cause no problem. The moment the steering wheel is turned, say to the left, the wheels on the right-hand side of the vehicle are having to travel a greater distance around the arc than those on the left. This will tighten up the transmission considerably as both axles and all the wheels are forced to rotate at differing speeds. That is transmission wind-up. Long term, this will lead to severe tyre wear and eventual damage to the gearbox. Changing gear is difficult with transmission wind-up. This situation does not arise off road because of the type of terrain. Muddy, wet or stony surfaces will allow wheel slip without the driver knowing and this will cancel out any potential wind-up.

The design of permanent FWD vehicles therefore needed careful consideration of transmission wind-up. The problem was dealt with by installing a third differential. Whilst the other two are located, respectively, on front and rear axles this additional one is inside the gearbox. It allows both axles' wheels to rotate at different speeds. However, if one axle's wheel revolves faster than the other while driving off road in slippery conditions this *centre differential* will permit the drive to go the easiest route – the power will go to the axle that can spin its wheels most freely. This is the last thing you want because if you have one wheel on a slippery surface and the other three wheels on firmer ground everything transfers to that one wheel (Fig. 1.4). Thus, all permanent FWD vehicles are equipped with a centre differential lock on that central differential. This has the effect of stopping the centre differential working so that drive will be equalised between the front and rear axles. This lock should be in the 'lock' position when on slippery surfaces and off road but unlocked whenever driving on dry, hard surfaces.

The term 'diff. lock' has a magical sound to an off-road enthusiast but, in this case, it only puts the vehicle in the same locked-up mode as other vehicles with FWD engaged whilst off road. It has no other function. *Axle differential locks* are a different bag of tricks altogether. These locks are fitted to the front and rear differentials and when engaged can give a startling performance in extreme off-road conditions. The mechanics are the same as for the centre differential lock. Normally, if one of the two wheels on an axle loses grip and begins to spin, all power is transferred across to that spinning wheel from the one that did have grip. Thus one wheel losing traction will affect the whole axle, putting it out of action. The 'axle diff. lock', however, will equalise the power so that the wheels rotate at the same speed. The locks are not usually fitted as standard to off-road vehicles (Mercedes and Toyota VX Land Cruiser excepted) and can be expensive.

There are some problems with using them. When activated on the front axle, steering can be difficult. An experienced person would find them beneficial but, as with all off roading, the conditions ahead must be read carefully so that the locks can be engaged when required. Locking them after you have got into trouble will probably compound the difficulty rather than help. The Australian company ARB manufacture axle differential locks which are operated by compressed air. Front and rear locks are separate and so the driver can select which axles are to be locked.

Some vehicles may be fitted with what is termed a limited slip differential. Remember, the job of a differential is to allow one wheel to travel at a different speed to the other on the same axle. When a limited slip device is fitted this still allows an imbalance of wheel speeds but when spinning of one wheel occurs the differential will lock, through a series of clutch plates, resulting in both wheels being driven.

Freewheeling hubs

These are only fitted when the vehicle has part-time FWD. Whilst driving in only two-wheel drive the front prop shaft becomes disconnected so that no drive goes to the front wheels. However, as the front wheels rotate so the half-shafts, front differential and prop shaft rotate as they are still connected. The friction from this dead weight will increase fuel consumption and increase wear on these parts. When disengaged the free-wheeling hubs will disconnect the wheel from the half-shaft (and therefore the diff. and prop shaft). Now, when the wheel rotates it does so freely, reducing wear and decreasing fuel consumption. Most are manual hubs which means that they have to be disengaged and engaged by hand. This usually entails turning a knob on the end of the hub to a 'locked' or 'unlocked' position. Some Japanese manufacturers now supply automatic hubs that lock on engaging FWD. New vehicles normally have hubs fitted as standard. Older ones can have manual freewheeling hubs

Above: Fig. 1.5 Driving beyond the limits of the suspension travel
Below: Fig. 1.6 This shows the considerable wheel articulation essential in maintaining contact with the ground

Above: Fig. 1.7   The approach angle of this 4x4 will be sufficient to enable the vehicle to begin the climb without the front bumper striking the ground
Below: Fig. 1.8   The departure angle – just made it!

fitted. Always remember to lock hubs prior to engaging FWD as not doing so can cause transmission problems (as well as not giving FWD).

The transmission brake

Not all off-road vehicles are fitted with transmission brakes; this feature is limited, essentially, to all Land Rover vehicles, early Suzuki models and the latest Nissan GR Patrols. There is a housing for the brake located around the rear prop shaft where it emerges behind the gearbox. Even when the vehicle is in neutral the rear prop shaft will rotate when the wheels move. Consequently, by locking the prop shaft with a hand-operated brake the rear wheels will be prevented from moving. Thus the handbrake does not work directly on the rear brake drums as in most vehicles but off a second system that will be independent from the wheels. The advantages of this when off roading soon become apparent after wading in water. With the brake drums or discs wet no efficient braking system is available: unless you have a transmission brake!

Axles

A live axle is a tube with a wheel at either end. The differential and drive shafts are encased in that tube. A dead axle is found on independently-sprung systems. The differential is remotely located with open drive shafts to each wheel.

Suspension

The suspension on a FWD vehicle is important not just for the ride and comfort but because drive control is determined off road by that suspension. The basic form can be seen, for instance, on the Land Rover prior to around 1981/2. This is a leaf spring type commonly known as 'cart springs'. These are layers of steel strips with an eye at each end which connect with the chassis through a shackle plate and pin. The axle, which is live, is located at right angles across the centre of the two springs. The fundamental feature of this type of spring is that it holds the axle in place (see Fig. 1.9).

Coil suspension can come in two forms. The first, attached one each side of a live axle, acts as a spring only and has to be located separately with a longitudinal articulating bar. These are on both sides of the chassis (see Fig. 1. I 0). A second method of attaching a coil-sprung live axle is a three point 'A' frame.

There are advantages and disadvantages with all systems. The simple and rugged leaf springs produce a harder ride and have less

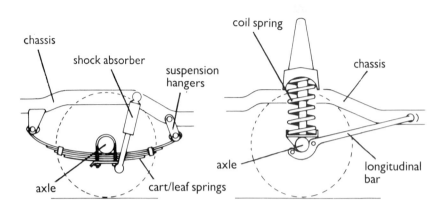

fig. 1.9 Leaf spring suspension, which also holds the live axle in place

Fig. 1.10 Coil suspension with longitudinal bar to hold live axle in place

axle travel than most coil suspension designs. These latter forms give a softer ride and better axle travel but require additional rubber-bushed locating bars.

Much is said, both for an against, the plethora of replacement shock absorbers on the market that can be used instead of the vehicle manufacturer's own part. They can be three times the price but may improve the ride on and off road. It is the inner construction that puts up the price. De Carbon of France invented the technology of the monotube dual gas/oil system shock absorber, and their design is copied throughout the world. The gas is located at the lower end of the shock absorber and is physically separated from the oil above by a free piston. It is this oil that contains the floating-valve piston, which soaks up the bumps and, hopefully, keeps all four wheels on the ground by its instant response. The design differs from the conventional telescopic unit in three ways: it has a single tube, which helps in dissipating heat; there is physical separation of oil and air, which prevents aeration of the oil; and it is permanently pressurised, which helps to keep the system simple and prevents the need for complex valves and, ultimately, helps the hydraulic fluids to remain homogenous.

Suspension travel and wheel articulation

This refers to the distance the axle travels between its lowest and uppermost points. The greater the movement the more chance of keeping all wheels in contact with the ground, thus maintaining traction and forward movement (see Fig. 1.5).

Fig. 1.6 shows axle articulation on this particular vehicle pushed almost to its limit. If this is pushed slightly further a cross-axle situation will arise, in which diagonally opposed wheels will spin freely in the air. This phenomenon could be remedied in vehicles fitted with cross-axle differential locks. However, this condition of cross axles can be avoided by selective driving techniques. (See Chapter 4.)

Approach and departure angles

This is best explained by looking at Figs 1.7 and 1.8. The 4x4, especially with the ability afforded by the low ratio gears, allows a very steep incline to be attempted. However, the vehicle has to approach (or leave) that incline. The closer the wheels are to the ends of the vehicle the better it is, because a steeper incline angle can be approached. If there is an extended bumper at the front then the angle that can be approached will be lower. On a steep incline

Fig. 1.11 This Land Rover has reached its Ramp Breakover Angle, and the wheels are not making sufficient traction on the ground to move it

the bumper will just bury itself into the ground at the bottom of the slope. A vehicle's approach angle is often higher than the departure angle, particularly with regard to long wheelbase models. As the vehicle reaches flat terrain after descending a steep slope the front will straighten out and the back of the vehicle comes low to the ground. The longer the body overhang at the rear, the greater likelihood there is that it will hit the ground, even lifting the rear wheels off the ground. Tow bars can also affect the rear ground clearance and seriously restrict departure angles.

Ramp breakover angle and ground clearance

Crossing very rough ground strewn with boulders and rocks can be a bit noisy (and expensive!) if your vehicle has a low ground clearance. But too much emphasis can be placed on the height of axles above the ground. Remember that too much height will affect the centre of gravity making the vehicle unstable. It is more important to consider the 'ramp breakover angle'. This relates to the angle of a ridge that can be attempted without grounding the belly of the vehicle on that ridge (see Figs. 1.11 and 1.12). The distance between the front and rear wheels is the factor governing the ramp breakover angle. The shorter the wheelbase the less likely a grounding out will occur.

Fig. 1.12 Skills required off road are very different to those on road!

2

What 4x4?

The range of FWD vehicles grow annually. During 1992, when the rest of the automotive industry was suffering from a growing recession, the 4x4 models were selling at a steady 10% increase on previous years. In this chapter we will look at the more popular makes suitable for off-road work. Performance 4x4 saloon cars do not fit this category and have been excluded. Vehicles suitable for expeditions are dealt with in further detail in Chapter 9.

AUVERLAND

Auverland S.A. evolved from the French company SIMI. They were responsible for the Cournil four-wheel drive vehicles such as the UMM. With such a pedigree it was inevitable that they would develop a rugged off-roeader. For almost eight years the French government have used the Auverland A3 for military and gendarmerie use. Exports slowly percolated through to other European countries, and by 1990 it was becoming established in the UK. With an approach angle of 57 degrees, a good ground clearance and an agile ability off road that instils confidence it really seems as if this vehicle was built by an off-roader. Its utilitarian feel puts it squarely within the UMM and hard top Land Rover group. The box-section, ladder-framed, chassis has long-travel coil springs and live axles which provide impressive articulation. The drive and transmission, like its predecessors, comes from Peugeot. The vehicle is relatively lightweight so that the rather modest power output produces a reasonable performance when driven hard. Four-wheel drive is part-time and the transfer box is controlled by two levers, for high and low ratio. Recent models now have power-assisted steering. Chrome-plated 16-in spoked steel rims come with Michelin XM&S4 tyres as standard. The maximum towing weight is 550 kg unbraked and 1250 kg when braked. The 1.9-litre Peugeot, naturally-aspirated, indirect injection diesel

VEHICLES AT A GLANCE

	P'up	Estate	H/Top	Diesel	Petrol			Wbase
Auverland	*	*	*	1.9lt	65bhp			2250
Dacia Duster		*	*		N/A	1.4lt	65bhp	
Daihatsu Fourtrak	*	3dr	*	2.8lt	72bhp		N/A	2205
				101bhpTDi				2530
						2800		
Daihatsu Sportrak		3dr	*		N/A	1.6lt	94bhp	2175
Fiat Panda 4x4		2dr			N/A	1.0lt	52bhp	
Ford Maverick/Nissan		3dr		2.7ltr	100bhp	2.4lt	124bhp	2450
Terrano 11		5dr						2650
Isuzu Trooper		3dr	*	3.0lt	113bhp	3.2lt	174bhp V6	2330
		5dr						2760
Jeep Wrangler		2dr			N/A	2.5lt	122bhp	2373
						4.0lt	184bhp	
Jeep Cherokee		4dr			N/A	2.5lt	122bhp	2576
						4.0lt	184bhp	
Lada Niva		3dr			N/A	1.6lt	80bhp	2235
Land Rover Defender	*	3dr	*	2.5lt	68bhp	2.5lt	83bhp	2360
		5dr		2.5lt	107bhp TDi	3.5lt	134bhp V8	2794
								3226
L. R. Discovery		3/5dr		2.5lt	111bhp TDi	3.5lt	153bhp V8	2540
						2.0lt	134bhp	2540
Range Rover		5dr	*	2.5lt	111bhp TDi	3.9lt	182bhp V8	2540
						4.2lt	200bhp V8	2743
Mahindra	*	3dr	*	2.1lt	60bhp		N/A	2311
				2.5lt	76bhp			2426
Mercedes G-Wagen		3dr		3.0lt	113bhp	3.0lt	170bhp	2400
		5dr						2850
Mitsubishi Shogun		3dr		2.5lt	98bhp	3.0lt	147bhp V6	2420
		5dr						2725
Mitsubishi L200	*			2.5lt	68bhp	2.0lt	92bhp	2680
Nissan Patrol		2dr		2.8lt	114bhp	3.0lt	135bhp	2380
		4dr						3000
Nissan GR		5dr		4.2lt	110bhp	4.2lt	170bhp	2970
Nissan D21	*			2.5lt	75bhp	2.4lt	100bhp	2950
S-D-P Pinzgauer			*	2.4lt	115bhp TDi		N/A	2400
4x4 & 6x6								2690
Suzuki Samurai		2dr	*		N/A	1.3lt	63bhp	2030
								2375
Suzuki Vitara		3/5dr			N/A	1.6lt	74bhp	2200
						80 & 95bhp		2480
Toyota Land Cruiser II	*	3dr		2.5lt	88bhp		N/A	2310
Toyota Land Cruiser VX		5dr		4.2lt	165bhp TD		N/A	2850
Toyota HiLux	*			2.5lt	81bhp	2.2lt	92bhp	2840
UMM Alter	*	3/5dr	*	2.5lt	76bhp &		N/A	2560
					110bhp			3078
				TDi				
Vauxhall Frontera Sport		3			N/A	2lt	110bhp	2330
Vauxhall Frontera		5dr		2.3lt	96bhp	2.4lt	120bhp	2760
Vauxhall Brava	*			2.5lt	72bhp	2.3lt	89bhp	3025
Volkswagen Tristar	*	*		1.6lt	70bhp	2.1lt	112bhp	2840

produces a maximum power output of 65 bhp at 4,600 rpm with torque of 88 lb/ft at 2,070 rpm.

DACIA

Relative newcomers to the market in the early 1980s, these Rumanian vehicles have not really proved themselves off road and have a limited ground clearance. They are available as either the Duster GLX three-door estate or Duster Roadster, a three-door convertible. There are two power options. The first vehicles arrived in the UK with a 1.4-litre petrol engine delivering 65 bhp at 5,250 rpm. Torque is 77 lb/ft at 3,000 rpm. By 1990 the GLD diesel model was available. This unit is the Renault 1596 cc F8M engine, which develops 56 bhp at 4,800 rpm and 74 lb/ft of torque at 2,250 rpm. The suspension has a live rear axle on leaf springs and independent front. They are a part-time 4x4 with a maximum towing weight of 1,270 kg. Resale values are not especially good. A cheap and cheerful off roader!

DAIHATSU

The Daihatsu motor manufacturers are the oldest such company in Japan and have been affiliated with Toyota since 1967. They began with three-wheeled vehicles back in the early 1930s, and their first 4x4s appeared in 1974. Daihatsu broke into the off-road market in much the same way as Suzuki. Both started with small commercial vehicles suitable for the developing world but aimed particularly at South East Asia. These early models were also bought and modified by customers in the leisure market, and so began the subsequent evolution to the modern Fourtrak. It has established an excellent reputation, especially with the comfortable estate versions. All versions have part-time FWD. The short wheelbase measures, approximately, 100 in between axles, the long wheelbase is 112 in. All have three doors and are capable of towing up to 3,500 kg. The suspension consists of live axles on leaf springs.

The present Fourtrak model range consists of soft or hard top utility and estate. There are three engines available. The 1998 cc petrol, produces 87 bhp at 4,600 rpm, 116 lb/ft at 3,000 rpm whilst the basic 2765 cc diesel gives 72 bhp at 3,800 rpm, 124 lb/ft at 2,200

rpm. The turbocharged, intercooled version gives 100 bhp at 3,400 rpm, and 162 lb/ft at 2,200 rpm.

The Sportrak model was introduced during the spring of 1989. With a length of 145 in, it is similar to the Fourtrak but is more of a lightweight. The early SOHC 1589 cc petrol engine gave 84 bhp at 6,000 rpm and torque of 92 lb/ft at 3,500 rpm. It can give a more brisk acceleration than the Fourtrak and is easier to handle off road. With its growing success, the eventual line up includes at the top of the range a 16-valve injection model, complete with catalytic converter, producing a boosted power output to 94 bhp at 5,700 rpm.

Secondhand Daihatsu Vehicles

The first Daihatsu 4x4 was the F10 in 1974 and was built for cheap robustness. The ladder-frame chassis had galvanised body parts and was driven by a 58 bhp, 1 litre petrol engine, extracted from its saloon car range. FWD was selectable and the suspension had semi-elliptic springs. The model which reached the UK and soon became popular was the F20. Towards the end of the 1970s a number of versions were available, including short and long wheelbase formats, and had cornered 20% of the country's 4x4 market. They represented fairly basic commercial vehicles, as pickups and hard or soft tops. Two engine variants were possible, both more powerful than the F10, which was slowly phased out. The 1587cc petrol engine produced around 66 bhp at 4,800 rpm whilst the 2538 cc diesel engine produced 62 bhp.

The F10 & 20 were based on an, almost, 80-in wheelbase, but in the 1980s the Fourtrak was born, developed around a wider track and a 87-in wheelbase. Later, the estate version was produced, accommodating seven people in a 100-in wheelbase vehicle that was, characteristically, stepped in the centre for more rear space. Typically, these came in two-tone paintwork. New for 1988 was the turbo-diesel engine, running faster and quieter than the previous naturally-aspirated engine. At this stage it produced 90 bhp although this was boosted to 100 bhp by the early 1990s.

Illustrations, facing page:
Top: *Fig. 2.1   The Auverland – here equipped for trialling*
Centre: *Fig. 2.2   Daihatsu Fourtrak*
Bottom: *Fig. 2.3   Daihatsu Sportrak EL (photo by Daihatsu UK Ltd)*

FIAT

Although a very limited off roader, especially in load carrying, the Panda 4x4 has a considerable cult following. In Italy it is used extensively in very difficult terrain, and a number of Saharan expeditions have also used this three-door hatchback. In fact, there have been more Fiat Panda 4x4s sold in Europe than any other FWD vehicle. It has part-time FWD and can tow up to 900 kg. The early 900 cc petrol engine delivers 48 bhp at 5,600 rpm with torque of 51 lb/ft at 3,500 rpm but it was later replaced by a 1-litre FIRE engine. The suspension has a live rear axle on leaf springs and independent front.

FORD

Ford has not been renowned in Europe as a manufacturer of a four-wheel drive vehicle but in its home country it forms a fundamental part of the line up. The Ford Ranger pickup is one of the best-selling vehicles in America, whilst the Explorer is branded as the great family estate vehicle. The Ford Bronco has been around in its various gutsy guises since the 1970s and has a specification comparable with the Range Rover.

Ford has been one of the obvious exceptions in the European 4x4 market, but with the decline in 2x4 vehicles at the start of the 1990s it has followed the line of several other manufacturers – combining the development of such a vehicle with an existing 4x4 company. In the early summer of 1993 the Ford Maverick is being released following several years work with Nissan on the project. For detail, see the Nissan Terrano 11 on page 42. At the present time there is some concern over the different marketing policies of the two companies as well as the price of spares. Typically, Japanese vehicles have a much higher cost which is reflected in the insurance rates. Time will tell!

Illustrations, facing page:
Top: *Fig. 2.4   A 1993 model Isuzu Trooper LWB*
Centre: *Fig. 2.5   Lada Niva – a thoroughbred off roader, in action*
Bottom: *Fig. 2.6   Jeep Wrangler (Courtesy of Chrysler Jeep Imports UK)*

ISUZU

Although one of the automotive giants around the world, the Japanese company Isuzu was the last of the Far Eastern countries to launch a luxury 4x4 on to the expanding and lucrative UK market. It has always had some connections with the UK market. In the earliest days the company was licensed to build Wolseleys and later, in 1953, they produced the Hillman Minx. When General Motors took a slice of the company in 1971 the marketing of their vehicles became a joint policy which is displayed in a number of models, not least the connection with Vauxhall's Frontera project.

Isuzu have always been primarily concerned with commercial vehicles. The hard top Isuzu van has been well established in Europe and Africa for some time, but it was only recently, in 1987, that the refined Trooper was introduced even though it was available elsewhere in 1981. Competing head-on with the Mitsubishi Shogun, the Trooper shared an almost identical layout of transmission and suspension. The styling was more reminiscent of its commercial heritage as was the solid chassis. International Motors, who import the Trooper, priced the vehicle so astutely that the vehicle became an instant success. The vehicle had already been around for several years on the continent and, particularly, in Australia. The latter country has been the principal market for Isuzu, so that even Land Rovers are now produced there using the Isuzu diesel engine. The Trooper had won accolades of top 4x4 before ever reaching the European shores. By the time the replacement model had been introduced in 1992 the vehicle had the reputation as one of the most reliable 4x4s.

Current Isuzu Models

The short and long wheelbase Troopers introduced in 1992 were a significant step up in specification from the earlier models. The petrol version possesses a 3.2 litre, 24-valve, twin overhead cam, V6 Efi engine which can produce 174 bhp at 5,200 rpm and a torque value of 192 lb/ft at 3,750 rpm. The turbocharged, intercooled diesel is a four-cylinder, 3.1 litre indirect injection unit that develops 113 bhp at 3,600 rpm and 192 lb/ft torque at 2,000 rpm. The transmission is part-time. The front suspension consists of independent double wishbones with torsion bars and gas-filled shock absorbers. The rear still retains the live axle with leaf springs from the previous model, but has three trailing links and a Panhard rod. Towing capacity remains at 3,000 kg.

The three equipment levels are retained with the highest, Citation model, having air conditioning, anti-lock brakes, limited slip rear differential, power steering with tilt adjustment and many hidden electric motors, including electric-heated, foldable mirrors which can be tucked out of the way just before off roading.

Secondhand Troopers

The Isuzus all show considerable luxury and comfort with power steering as standard. The Trooper is available in short and long wheelbase forms. All have part-time FWD, 3,000 kg towing capability and good engine braking in low range. The rear suspension is of a live axle on leaf springs whilst the front is independent using wishbone and torsion bars. The first vehicles arriving in the UK were limited to either a 2.25 litre petrol or an under-powered 2.2 turbo-diesel. The former unit produced a reasonable 108 bhp at 4,600 rpm, with a torque of 123 lb/ft at 2,600 rpm. The diesel on the other hand produced 74 bhp at 4,000 rpm and 114 lb/ft at 2,500 rpm. Both engines had four cylinders. A year after their first introduction new engine options arrived. A second petrol option became available in the form of a 2559 cc fuel-injected engine that delivered 111 bhp at 5,000 rpm but produced a better torque figure of 138 lb/ft at 2,500 rpm. The low-powered diesel engine was replaced by a 2771 cc diesel unit capable of 95 bhp at 3,800 rpm, yielding 153 lb/ft at 2,500 rpm. With the introduction of the more powerful engines the ratios on the gearing were changed to provide for a higher top gear. In addition, the clutch was uprated to accommodate the increase in torque. Automatic free-wheeling hubs are present on all models. Out of all the luxury 4x4 vehicles available, the Trooper is probably, from new, the one most often used off road.

The vehicles are available in three levels of trim: from the basic, which includes power steering, up to their Citation model. This top-of-the-range vehicle includes limited slip differential, air conditioning and cruise control on the petrol engines. The intermediate model, (heavy) Duty Pack, was intended to provide options that the serious off roader could use such as high-pressure headlight cleaning and the limited slip differential.

JEEP

With an eighty-strong dealer network setup in January 1993, the range of Jeeps were set to take the British by storm. Prior to this, the Wrangler model had been accessible only through a limited number of entrepreneurs and by personal import. The evolution from a primordial military machine to America's favourite sport utility has taken fifty years and has moved between several companies. Kaiser Industries took over the development of the Jeep in 1953 from Willys-Overland and produced the civilian vehicle, the CJ Series. The American Motors Corporation (AMC) took on the CJ in 1970 as part of their leisure line-up, but it was not until 1987, when it was sold to the Chrysler Corporation, that exports were augmented. Some years prior to this, AMC had been bought out by Renault and this gave them the opportunity to sell the CJ Series through some of the French dealers. This has led its cult following to expand within Europe, and a number of specific Jeep clubs have sprung up in France and Germany. Chrysler will be hoping to sell 16,000 units per year in the UK by the end of the decade.

Essentially, there are three models to consider, although each has its own complex range that can be confusing. The Wrangler, which replaced the CJ-7 back in 1987, is the direct descendant of the original Willys Jeep and until recent years had changed little. The angular body still retains the leaf-sprung suspension, although now much improved on the earlier CJs. By 1990, the Wrangler had changed to become the Jeep Renegade. The engines in these base models had grown steadily over the decades, from a V6 in the 1960s, through to a guzzling 5-litre V8 in the 1970s. With the economical 1980s came the option of either a 4-cylinder, 2.5-litre injection or a 6-cylinder, 4.2-litre carburettor engine. Both delivered modest power, 117 bhp and 114 bhp respectively. The Renegade came with the latest 4-litre, 170 bhp injection engine.

Illustrations, facing page:
Top: *Fig. 2.7   Jeep Cherokee 4.0 (Courtesy Chrysler Jeep Imports UK)*
Centre: *Fig. 2.9   Range Rover with a 1948 80-in Land Rover for restoration: still an obtainable classic*
Bottom: *Fig. 2.10   A well equipped Land Rover 90 Diesel; NB high-air intake, lights and winch*

The second model, and one that has always meant comfort and space, has been the XJ Cherokee series. With a million vehicles produced over six years at the Toledo plant, up until 1990, this is the most successful Jeep produced. The 4-cylinder, 2.5-litre and the 6-cylinder, 4-litre engines were mainly for the home market. Those seen on the Continent are powered, principally, by the Renault 2.1-litre turbocharged diesel engine. The luxurious Cherokee Ltd model, introduced into the UK in 1993, has a 4-litre engine capable of 184 bhp at 4,750 rpm and torque of 214 lb.ft at 3,950 rpm.

Chrysler took America by storm when they announced the Grand Cherokee at the Detroit Motor Show in 1992. Due in the UK in 1994, it is set to compete head on with the Discovery and Range Rover. The likelihood is that it will arrive with the Magnum V8 Efi engine (producing 220 bhp at 4,800 rpm and 285 lb.ft at 3,600 rpm), capable of towing a massive 6,500 lbs. Optional with this will be heavy duty radiator, auxiliary transmission cooler and 3.73 axle ratios.

Secondhand Jeeps

Both of the Wrangler and of Cherokee 1980 models can be found but they may have a variety of power units depending on their original source. Both have part-time four-wheel drive with automatic transmission options. The Wrangler has leaf springs, telescopic shock absorbers and anti-roll bar. The Cherokee has coil sprung suspension with gas-filled shock absorbers and anti-roll bar. Wheels are 15-in steel or alloy rims. Engine options vary: the 2.5-litre, 4-cylinder in-line, petrol injection produces 117 bhp at 5,000 rpm and torque of 141 lb/ft at 3,500 rpm; the 4.2-litre, 6-cylinder in-line, carburettor engine produces 114 bhp at 3,000 rpm and torque of 210 lb/ft at 2,000 rpm; and the 4.0-litre, 6-cylinder in-line, petrol injection produces 177 bhp at 4,500 rpm and torque of 224 lb/ft at 2,500 rpm.

KIA

As yet, the 4x4 produced by the oldest Korean auto manufacturer has only been in production since early 1993. The Kia Sportage is set to challenge the superiority of the Japanese vehicles and the exact arrival date in the UK is an unknown factor. Weighing in at 1,390 kg, the Sportage fits within the Vitara-Frontera category and has a Mazda twin overhead camshaft 2-litre engine which develops 140 bhp and 126 lb/ft of torque at 6,000 rpm.

LADA

The basic Niva model is a spartan three-door hatchback from the CIS. Since first arriving in the UK in 1979 they have changed little. It has permanent FWD, and a 1570 cc petrol engine delivering 78 bhp at 5,400 rpm. Torque is 88 lb/ft at 3,000 rpm and it can tow a maximum of 1,500 kg. The independent suspension has a wishbone at the front and a live axle on coil springs at the rear. The 16-in wheels provide a 9-in ground clearance.

Nivas have been extensively tried and tested, and it is the basic hire car in Iceland. It is a good off roader at an affordable price. The top of the model range is the Niva Cossak with more extras and better trim. There is also a rare Cabriolet version.

LAND ROVER

A company with a formidable record and a name synonymous with off roading. The present range consists of vehicles all with permanent FWD and a maximum towing capacity of 4,000 kg. They have good ground clearance with amazing wheel articulation. Three main groups of vehicles are currently in production: the Defender, the Discovery and the Range Rover.

The Defender, in either the 90-in or 110-in wheelbase form, is the basic Land Rover with the long lineage from 1948. For many the Defender 90 is the *real* off-road machine, with few rivals. The Defender 110 has the wider range of body options including the twelve-seater, five-door station wagon. The engine most commonly seen in the Defender is the 200 series TDi, originally designed for the Discovery. The 2.5 turbocharged engine yields 108 bhp at 3800 rpm and torque of 188 lb/ft at 1,800 rpm. Coupled with a gearbox with new ratios the combination is a formidable off-road vehicle. The 4-cylinder, 2.5 cc petrol engine (83 bhp at 4,000 rpm, 133 lb/ft at 2,000 rpm) is available to order, and the powerful, but very thirsty, 3528 cc V8 petrol is still an option with 134 bhp at 4,000 rpm, and 187 lb/ft at 2,500 rpm.

Towards the end of 1989 Land Rover introduced their first all-new vehicle for nineteen years. Called the Discovery, it was designed to meet the Japanese competition head-on and fills the gap between the basic Land Rover and luxury Range Rover. The TDi engine puts out 111 bhp at 4,000 revs and has a top speed around 92 mph. The

Fig. 2.11   A 1985 Range Rover Vogue on expedition

Fig. 2.12   A 30-year-old Land Rover Series 2A after a rebuild, and with plenty of life left

Fig. 2.13 A Land Rover Discovery TDi, trialling

converse of the Range Rover, far fewer petrol versions of the Discovery have been produced. The early vehicles had the carburetted petrol 3.5-litre V8 engine but due to poor fuel consumption it was soon replaced by the Efi 3.5 V8. This gives 153 bhp at 4,750 rpm and 190 lb/ft at 3000 rpm.

During 1993 the Discovery Mpi was introduced fitted with the Rover T16 two litre petrol engine as found in the Rover 800 range. This 16-valve unit with overhead camshaft, hydraulic tappets and multipoint petrol injection also features a distributorless quad-coil ignition system which in all produces 134 bhp at 6,000 rpm. At the same time, Land Rover introduced the Commercial Discovery based on the 3-door TDi model capable of a 679 kilogram payload.

During 1992 the Range Rover came of age. Twenty-one years from its original development the vehicle has, outwardly, changed very little and still remains the standard to which many manufacturers aim.

Technologically, it is a totally different machine from the early models although it has always been maintained as a superb off roader with class. Barely 5% of the vehicles produced in 1992 were diesel powered. The VM indirect injection 2.5 Turbo engine was

changed that year for the direct injection 200 TDi engine used in the Discovery. Diesel is available in the lowest spec models and produces 111 bhp at 4,000 rpm with torque of 195 lb/ft at 1,800 rpm. The 3.9 Efi engine gives a gutsy 185 bhp at 4,750 rpm with 235 lb/ft at 2,600 rpm. This engine is available in either the Vogue or SE models. Late in November 1992 the extended wheelbase, LSE model, was released. The all-aluminium water-cooled V8 Efi engine in this vehicle is 4.2 litres with a maximum power output of 200 bhp at 4,850 rpm and torque of 250 lb/ft at 3,250 rpm. All the current models use a Borg Warner chain-driven two-speed transfer case which incorporates a viscous-controlled centre differential. The suspension consists of live axles with anti-roll bars and hydraulic dampers. The LSE, with its 2,743 mm wheelbase, is fitted with an electronically-controlled air suspension which features a set of variable-rate air springs so that the front and rear is automatically self-levelling. The ventilated front and plain rear disc brakes on the Range Rovers have full ABS, and the LSE supports an electronic traction control system on the rear axle.

Secondhand Land Rovers

In the UK Land Rovers have been available in large numbers for considerably longer than other four-wheel drive vehicles. Early models can be purchased cheaply and make a good 4x4 with which to start.

The first Land Rovers were produced in 1948 and had an 80-in wheelbase. They were powered by a 1.6-litre engine that produced 50 bhp at 4,000 rpm and torque of 80 lb/ft at 2,000 rpm. This early Series One stayed almost the same until 1952 when the engine capacity was raised to 2 litres, giving 52 bhp and a much higher torque value of 101 lb/ft. 1954 saw an increase in wheelbase to 86

Illustrations, facing page:
Top: *Fig. 2.14   Ex-army Land Rover lightweight*
Centre: *Fig. 2.15   A modified 110 Land Rover, a twin cab diesel*
Bottom: *Fig. 2.16   100 in hybrid: Range Rover donor vehicle with chassis cut off behind rear wheels; body parts from Land Rover 109 and 110; Rover V8 engine from Rover P6 car; heavy duty coil suspension with 4-way shocks; ARB air-locking differentials on both axles – just to name a few modifications! (Courtesy of* International Off-Roader)

in but with the same engine. In 1957 the wheelbase was further extended to 88 in so that a diesel engine could be accommodated.

A second model, the 107-in long wheelbase, was introduced during 1954 which, later, was also stretched another two inches. It was a ten seater and looked as though it had been bolted together like a kit. All of these Series One models were available with either a canvas top or hard top. Those with side windows were called station wagons and were perhaps the forerunner of the modern three-door hatchback!

Land Rover introduced the reshaped Series Two model in 1958. This was available in short (88-in) or long wheelbase (109-in) forms. The petrol engine was bigger, uprated to 2286 cc. A 2052 cc diesel engine was now available. All possible configurations of top were optional on the Series Two, including a twelve-seater version. A Series 2A replaced the earlier series in 1962, and although it looked the same it had many improvements, especially in the transmission. A visual change came to the Series Two in 1968 due to an alteration in automotive legislation in several of the export countries. The headlights were moved to the wings.

The Series Three was released in 1971. The body was still very similar to previous models but there were many mechanical changes including an all-synchromesh gearbox, better axles and improved dashboard and heating system. As well as the 2.25-litre petrol and diesel engines a third, 6-cylinder engine with 83 bhp became available. This was discontinued in 1980 when the standard Rover V8, 3.5-litre petrol engine was fitted to a limited production run called the Stage 1 Land Rover. This was characterised by the extended bonnet, due to the repositioned radiator, necessary because of the increased size of engine. The V8 was only used in the 109 LWB vehicle and the engine was detuned to 91 bhp, although enthusiasts soon found ways of retuning the beast. The transmission was also changed to a full-time FWD.

Production of the Series Three lasted ten years until it was superseded by the 90 and 110 Land Rovers. The early vehicles were available in many body styles including three-door van, utility, or five-door, twelve-seater station wagons. All 90 and 110 vehicles were produced in a *luxury* County trim. After the mid-1980s the production of such a wide variety of models was severely reduced. Models also gained wind-down door windows, although the door-operated, courtesy light switch had to wait until 1990. The vehicles had been equipped from the start with improved power units. The engine blocks were increased to 2.5-litre and, with the increased size of the engine bay, there is plenty of space in which to work on them. The 4-cylinder, 2495 cc petrol engine now produced 83 bhp at 4,000 rpm and 133 lb/ft torque at 2,000 rpm. The 2495 cc diesel engine was later turbocharged to provide 85 bhp at 4,000 rpm with 150 lb/ft of torque at 1,800 rpm. The thirsty V8 was popular. This 3528 cc petrol engine produces 134 bhp at 4,000 rpm with 187 lb/ft of torque at 2,500 rpm, and it provides an excellent towing vehicle.

During the Land Rover production period many vehicles were made for military use only, but then became available on the secondhand market. The 88-in army lightweight has become very popular with Land Rover enthusiasts. Developed in the early 1960s they were a stripped-down version of the 88-in model so that they could become air portable by the Wessex helicopter. Forward Control Land Rovers began life in civilian guise, appearing in the early 1960s as part of the Series 2A line up. They were virtually a 4x4 lorry with a payload of 30 cwt. Although they looked very different, they had much in common with the LWB Series Two. Originally with the standard 2.25-litre, 4-cylinder petrol engine, the 67 bhp was not really sufficient to drive the 2-ton vehicle. When the 6-cylinder petrol engine became available in 1966 the Forward Control 2B was released. Due to insufficient demand, production ceased in the early 1970s but a military version was developed instead, based on the new technology that was present in the form of the Range Rover. A new 101-in chassis bore the easily detachable panels so that it could be transported by the Wessex helicopter. Powered by the Range Rover V8 engine it shared the permanent four-wheel drive transmission. Around 2,000 were built between 1975 and 1978 but, during that time, no civilian use could be found. Once these vehicles were released from the army, the 101 FC gained an immediate cult following and their residual price remains high. In many ways it is an ideal expedition vehicle although one needs to be a true mechanical enthusiast to keep the beast roadworthy. Obtaining spares can be a problem as many of them were available only to the army.

Any of the early Land Rovers can be a practical vehicle for off-road transport. Over 200,000 Series One Land Rovers were built and more than a million Series Two and Three, worldwide. This reflects the wealth of secondhand spares that are easily obtainable. There are fewer 'green' vehicles than the Land Rover. Even new spares are comparatively cheap and readily available, except perhaps for some of the very early models. They may not be original Rover parts, as there are now a wide number of companies specialising in the manufacture of old Land Rover parts. Panels are of aluminium, which may eventually corrode through oxidation but at least will not rust, and other body parts are very strong, making it relatively easy to keep roadworthy. Owning an early Series One vehicle requires a sound mechanical knowledge, but it can be a sound investment. There are still a few 80-in models lying undiscovered in farmers' hillside barns although it is easy to pay through the nose for the base vehicle, especially as the plate number itself could be the most valuable item on the wreck. The 86-in Series One is an easier and more practical model as many later Land Rover parts will fit. Off roaders who are keen on trialling prefer this model because of its flat sides. Because Series Two and Three have waisted sides, they are not so easy to trial. Whatever vehicle you go for remember not to pay too much attention to the year. If it is three years older and in better condition it is probably worth more. Land Rovers sell on individual merit.

Of all the Land Rovers, Series Two models are amongst the lowest priced vehicles to be found. Despite an age of around thirty years, a careful examination may reveal a chassis stronger and more rust-free than a late Series Three. Even a novice could strip the vehicle to its basic chassis in a morning, although the rebuilding may take somewhat longer! In this way the rear cross-member and outriggers, common places for corrosion, can be replaced. The suspension hangers are another weak point on the chassis. The springs are easy to replace and are an almost inevitable problem. Poor leaf springs can be seen to bulge in the centre as the rust causes them to spread. Bulkheads are expensive to replace and being made of steel should be checked carefully for corrosion. The foot wells disintegrate quickly but replacement panels are cheap enough. The 2.25-litre petrol engine is the best unit to go for. We ran an expedition Land Rover with one of these for more than 200,000 miles with no engine overhaul and it never failed to start. It just took up smoking instead. Series Two gearboxes have produced fewer problems than early Series Three transmissions, and several of our Land Rover gearboxes have Series Two parts.

A particularly useful and common path to acquiring a good Land Rover is to buy two very cheap vehicles and build one from them. The second can be scrapped and used to recoup some of the costs. A good chassis may have a poor engine or body attached and vice versa. (See Fig 2.12.) This obviously requires some space and time but provides an ideal way of learning about the vehicle. It is rewarding and straightforward with plenty of literature available to help.

Secondhand Range Rovers
The first Range Rovers which rolled off the production line from 1971 changed comparatively little until the early 1980s. It was around 1984 when the curve in their graph of development really began to take off, as improved high compression V8 engines (3528 cc petrol with 127 bhp at 4,000 rpm, 194 lb/ft at 2,500 rpm) started to give moderately better economy. Late in 1985 the carburetted V8 was replaced by the Efi version, providing an increase in performance to 165 bhp at 4,500 rpm. The Vogue trim that had once been optional became the norm and a top model called the SE took over. With slippery leather seats it was steadily going up in the luxury stakes away from its off-roading origins. However, at no time was its off-road ability compromised, so that it became the ultimate air-conditioned, fast and comfortable touring vehicle. Also, during the mid-1980s the diesel option was added to the line up. This started with the VM 4-cylinder, 2.4-litre engine but was somewhat under-powered and was later replaced with the improved VM 2.5-litre unit. The former 2393 cc turbo diesel gives 112 bhp at 4,200 rpm, 183 lb/ft at 2,400 rpm, whilst the latter gives 119 bhp at 4,200 rpm with 209 lb/ft of torque at 1,950 rpm. By the end of the decade it was externally changed little, except for the Efi spoiler and anti-roll bars, but underneath the technology was radically new. The 3.5-litre engine was increased to 3.9 giving 185 bhp at 4,750 rpm and 235 lb/ft at 2,600 rpm. The transfer box also changed to incorporate viscous coupling on the differential lock.

HYBRIDS

As more and more secondhand 4x4 vehicles flood the market, there is much scope for the innovative few to construct their own off-road machine. Also there are clubs, e.g. AWDC where any vehicle is accepted so long as it abides by safety rules.

Now we are seeing Range Rover chassis with the advantage of disc brakes and coil suspension, topped with a Land Rover body. This will produce a 100-in wheelbase vehicle, a cross between a Land Rover 90-in and 110-in at half the cost. A visit to an AWDC modified trial will reveal an array of cut-down, shortened Rangers – some to 80-in wheelbases. It is also possible to purchase a coil sprung galvanised chassis to fit the older 88-in and 109-in wheelbase Land Rovers which can probably keep them going for another thirty years. The most common conversion is an engine change of some sort, either for more power or economy, and there is an infinite combination of power units and transmissions. There are numerous, cheap secondhand V8 engines, including SDi units, in the classified ads. A quick flick through a good off-road magazine will get you in touch with all the firms that supply the parts or who could do the job for you. (See page 207.)

Your main consideration when contemplating an engine conversion is: will the rest of the vehicle components be up to the extra power? For instance, it is asking a lot of a standard 2.25-litre Land Rover clutch to take the power of a Rover V8 engine. It is wise to seek advice from an expert. If you increase the top speed or weight of your vehicle you should be looking to up-rate the brakes and suspension.

Do not be put off by some of the complications, as most conversions have been done before and a phone call to one of the good engineering firms that advertise, will give you advice or the part you need. If you have done the work yourself, it would be wise to have the completed vehicle checked by a qualified engineer, for your safety, and that of the insurance company, who must be informed.

MAHINDRA

Reputedly the largest automotive manufacturer in India, Mahindra began producing a 4x4 during the 1980s based on the CJ3 Willys Jeep. Even though the company uses many of the original machine tools used by the Jeep Corporation, as it was then, they build the 4x4 under their own authority. A series of models have been produced with a steady improvement in specification. The present model produced by Mahindra is the Marksman and is based on a later CJ Jeep, although the technology is still based on 1970s development. The Marksman has a 95-in wheelbase and has a towing capacity of 1500 kg with a payload capacity of around 550 kg. As with the earlier versions, one of the power units available is the Peugeot 2.1-litre diesel engine. The more powerful 2.5-litre Peugeot diesel engine produces 76 bhp. The chassis is a steel, ladder frame with a suspension of semi-elliptical springs. The vehicle has a part-time four-wheel drive with high and low transfer ratio box. The Marksman is available as a truck cab, soft top and hard top.

MERCEDES

Surprisingly, Mercedes was very slow to hop on the leisure 4x4 bandwagon. After considerable development with the Austrian auto company Steyr-Daimler-Puch, who had experience with the Pinzgauer and Halflinger, the first vehicles appeared in 1979. From the start, they were designed to follow a line of quality machines and the Gëlandewagen was priced out of the market for the majority of

Fig. 2.17 A 3-door (SWB) Mercedes G-wagon

off roaders. Although strong comparisons were made with the Range Rover the vehicle has never really established itself in the UK market, despite the superb engineering build and pedigree. A wide range of models were produced including expensive soft-top versions and military options. Since its origin, the vehicle has outwardly changed little.

1991 saw the revamped Mercedes Gëlandewagen arrive in the UK. This high quality, but expensive, German competitor to the Range Rover had begun to match the latter vehicle every time a new model was announced. The previous G-Wagen was an impressive off roader and had part-time FWD. The latest specification includes permanent FWD and an optional self-levelling rear suspension. All models are capable of towing up to 2,800 kg except for the older 230 GE models which tow 2,500 kg. The new 300 series looks similar to its predecessor. The front grille is now coloured along with the rest of the body panels and the new bumpers are more rounded. Two engine formats are offered: the 300 GE and 300 GD. Both are equipped with the same 6-cylinder engines as the W124 series saloon cars. The 300 GE has the petrol 2960 cc version which has 170 bhp at 4,500 rpm, with torque of 173 lb/ft at 4,500 rpm. This vehicle also includes a catalytic converter. The 300 GD possesses the 113 bhp (at 4,600 rpm) diesel engine, derived from the same-sized block, and produces 141 lb/ft of torque at 2,800 rpm. The all-new transfer box has a manual differential lock, and ABS braking is present on all models.

Secondhand Vehicles

Older, secondhand Mercedes G-Wagen have the 200 series models as part of their line up. These are still available as new vehicles in the rest of Europe. All hold good secondhand value, particularly the 5-cylinder diesel model despite its limited power. The 230 GE has a 2299 cc petrol engine that produces 125 bhp at 5,100 rpm, with 142 lb/ft of torque at 4,000 rpm, whilst the beefier 280 GE has a 2746 cc petrol unit with 156 bhp at 5,250 rpm; the torque figure is 166 lb/ft at 4,250 rpm. The 300 GD, 2998 cc diesel, produces a very modest 88 bhp at 4,400 rpm, with 126 lb/ft at 4,500 rpm.

Except for the 230 GE, the Gëlandewagen is available with three-door or five-door options, which are the short and long wheelbase models. All have coil suspension with live axles along with an anti-roll bar. Both front and rear axles are fitted with cross-axle differential locks.

MITSUBISHI

The Shogun (known as the Pajero outside the UK) is a luxurious off-road machine from Japan, viewed by some as a less expensive competitor to the Range Rover. It was first introduced into the UK in 1983 and immediately became popular. The second generation models were a significant step up in technology and specification. With considerable back-up support the SWB Shogun has been modified to be used in rally-raid competitions. It finished in the top three places in the 8000-mile Paris-Cape Town Rally, and second in the Paris-Moscow-Beijing Rally.

Current Vehicles

There are two engine options on the current Shogun models. The 2477 cc turbocharged diesel engine produces 98 bhp at 4,200 rpm, with 177 lb/ft at 4,000 rpm. The alternative is a V6, 3-litre SOHC Efi petrol engine delivering 147 bhp at 5,000 rpm and torque of 174 lb/ft at 4,000 rpm. The transmission on all the Shoguns is a Super Select FWD. Designed to utilise the merits of both part-time and full-time FWD systems there is a front freewheel differential which allows for two- or four-wheel drive selection at any speed up to 62 mph. There is also a centre differential with viscous coupling which controls a standard 50:50 torque split as well as preventing transmission wind-up. Two-wheel drive can be selected to reduce drive resistance thus improving economy. In addition to these diff. locks there is also an electronically operated diff. lock on the rear axle to increase traction. The independent front suspension uses double wishbones and torsion bar springs. The rear axle possesses heavy coil springs. The braked towing capacities are 2,800 kg and 3,300 kg respectively, for the SWB and LWB.

The Diamond Option Packs (DOP) for the Shoguns vary for the two wheelbases. The SWB has anti-lock braking, remote control, variable rate suspension (a three-position switch to control the shock absorbers) and electronic compass/thermometer. These are also in the LWB DOP plus leather fascias/steering wheel and heated front seats with hydraulic suspension damping.

The L200 pickup range includes a FWD model and, like other Mitsubishi vehicles, is available with the Diamond Option Pack. This includes power steering, limited slip differential and heavy duty suspension.

Automatic freewheeling hubs and underbody protection guards are fitted as standard. The two engine options are a 2-litre petrol

Fig. 2.18   1993 Mitsubishi Shogun LWB (Courtesy of Colt Cars UK)

Fig. 2.19   Mitsubishi L200 4WD Pickup (Courtesy of Colt Cars UK)

unit (92 bhp at 5,500 rpm with 110 lb/ft torque produced at 3,500 rpm) and a 2.5-litre diesel (68 bhp at 4,200 rpm and 108 lb/ft at 2,000 rpm). The FWD model has a front suspension of double wishbones, torsion bars and a stabiliser bar. The rear suspension has a live axle with leaf springs. There are two wheelbases: 105.5-in and 116.1-in. The towing capacity for a braked trailer is 2,200 kg.

Secondhand vehicles

The previous Shogun models had a three-door, short wheelbase version, capable of towing around 2,800 kg, whilst the five-door, long wheelbase can achieve a maximum of 3,300 kg. The rear suspension of both is of a live axle on leaf springs type and the front is independent, using wishbone and torsion bars. The engines available are: 2555 cc petrol, 102 bhp at 4,500 rpm, 142 lb/ft at 2,500 rpm and a 2346 cc turbo diesel 84 bhp at 4,200 rpm, 133 lb/ft at 2,000 rpm. The later diesel has an intercooled turbo. In 1989 a V6 petrol model was introduced with all-round coil suspension.

NISSAN

The Patrol is another FWD from Japan. A good towing vehicle, it has a maximum pull of 3,500 kg. The three-door, short wheelbase version is still quite large at a length of 160 in, whilst the five-door, long wheelbase is positively huge at 188 in. This latter model is a seven-seater (all facing forward) in its estate format. Like most Japanese vehicles, the Patrol is good value for its luxury and extras. It has part-time FWD, power steering and limited slip differential. The suspension is of leaf springs, front and rear, supporting live axles. A drawback to the larger of the two vehicles is the long wheelbase, and the limited ramp-breakover-angle (see page 14) can produce difficulties on rocky, undulating terrain. Engines available are: 2753 cc petrol, 120 bhp at 4,800 rpm, 149 lb/ft at 3,200 rpm, and 3246 cc diesel, 95 bhp at 3,600 rpm, 160 lb/ft at 1,800 rpm.

Although it was introduced to continental Europe three years before, the GR Patrol did not arrive in the UK until 1992. This monster of a machine is still driven through a part-time four-wheel drive transmission but the suspension is coil sprung, front and rear to produce a very stable vehicle. This is aided by the width of over 1.8 metres. The petrol engine is very thirsty producing 170 bhp at 4,300 rpm, 236 lb/ft at 3,200 rpm whilst the diesel is still a good performer at 110 bhp at 4,000 rpm and a torque of 195 lb/ft at 2,000

rpm. The long wheelbase, 5-door option has length of 4.8 metres, longer than most other available 4x4 including the VX Land Cruiser. During 1993 a three-door model is being imported to the UK. A transmission brake is fitted on all GR Patrols, as are automatic freewheeling hubs.

The Terrano (also known as the Pathfinder) FWD model has been available on the Continent for several years, and in May 1993 the Terrano 11 arrived in the UK. Aimed to be a versatile all-roader vehicle, it is available with either SWB three-door or LWB five-door body options. The well tried and tested Nissan TD27T 2.7-litre turbo diesel engine (100 bhp at 4,000 rpm) and the 2.4-litre petrol engine (124 bhp at 5,200 rpm) are the power units available. The Terrano was designed in Europe as a European car and, to begin with, the production is held in Barcelona. The upper body has smooth lines whilst the lower portion is the rugged off-road section. FWD is selectable with a choice of high or low ratio gears. A limited slip differential is fitted as standard. At the front, the suspension is all-independent, with a double wishbone and torsion bar arrangement. At the rear, a coil-sprung live axle is controlled by a five-link system consisting of four trailing arms and a Panhard Rod.

SALAMANDER

Although it is not available at the time of publication, this company from Thailand are in the process of producing a 4x4 based on the Toyota 4Runner. It will be powered by the Toyota 2.5-litre, turbocharged diesel engine which is fitted to the Land Cruiser 2. However, the suspension will be that of the 4Runner with independent torsion bar on the front and coil springs on the rear live axle.

Illustrations, facing page:
Top: *Fig. 2.20 1984 model Nissan Patrol LWB*
Centre: *Fig. 2.21 Nissan Terrano 11 (Courtesy of Nissan Motor, GB)*
Bottom: *Fig. 2.22 Suzuki Vitara photographed whilst trialling*

SUZUKI

For many years the Japanese company Suzuki has specialised in the market for small off-road machines. The SJ series first appeared in 1982, in the form of the SJ410. This became the Santana Sport in 1987 when they were manufactured under licence in Spain. The SJ410 and the Santana have 970cc petrol engines (45 bhp at 5,500 rpm, 55 lb/ft at 3,000 rpm) whilst the SJ413, which arrived in 1985, has a 1361 cc petrol engine delivering power of 64 bhp and torque of 74 lb/ft maximum. FWD is part-time. All Suzukis are three-door and have little room for luggage if the rear seat is retained. The Samurai SWB tends to be somewhat pitchy on the road, and the LWB version, which is marginally better, was recently introduced to the UK. The LWB has a white resin hard top with sliding windows. The top is easily removed transforming it to a pickup. A 1.6-litre, 74 bhp petrol engine option is also now available. All have live axles suspended by leaf springs and are capable of towing a maximum of 1,100 kg.

In 1989 a totally new vehicle was introduced, the Vitara, with a length of 143 in. They originally had just a 1590 cc OHC petrol engine producing 74bhp at 5,250 rpm with torque of 90 lb/ft at 3,100 rpm. The latest catalytic engine option produces 80 bhp at 5,400 rpm and torque of 94 lb/ft at 3,000 rpm. The LWB, five-door model arrived in 1991 and with it came the single OHC, 16-valve Efi, 1590 cc engine, producing 95 bhp at 5,600 rpm and 98 lb/ft at 4,000 rpm. The towing maximum is the same as the other Suzukis. FWD is part-time.

TOYOTA

The sales of the Toyota Land Cruiser models in the UK have been somewhat disordered. Despite being one of the world's top selling 4x4s it was only available between 1975 and 1978 and then from 1981. Imported models were restricted to just one or two of the top, luxury vehicles.

Illustrations, facing page:
Top: *Fig. 2.23 A trialling Suzuki SJ*
Centre: *Fig. 2.24 Toyota Land Cruiser 2*
Bottom: *Fig. 2.25 Toyota VX Land Cruiser climbing a steep incline with ease*

45

Fig. 2.26 Toyota Hi-Lux

The Japanese FWD Toyota is well established throughout the world and has been since the early 1950s. In fact, they are the third largest automobile manufacturer, next to General Motors and Ford. Toyota began the development of its first post-war utility vehicle like its present-day, chief competitor, the Land Rover. The prototype BJ in 1950 closely resembled the Willys Jeep. However, for several decades the dominant 4x4 models have been the FJ Series, characteristically distinctive, some would say, ugly.

Up to four different wheelbase options were available, between 2.2 and 2.95 metres. These adaptable machines could be stripped down to a bare minimum of panels or converted into minibuses. Many of the present adventure FWD buses of Australia are based on an extended, tough FJ chassis. Body styling changed little during the 1960s and 1970s. The short wheelbase FJ25 and long wheelbase FJ45 came with either soft or hard top and the station wagon format. Only an occasional rare specimen of these FJs can be seen in the UK, although elsewhere in Europe, particularly Iceland, they may be more abundant than a Series Two or Three Land Rover.

It was the engine option which changed the most, although all were substantial power units. It was in 1980 that the greatest revision of the Series was made, to go up market as a competitor in the luxury leisure market. The FJ60V was a four-door station wagon with either a 4.2-litre petrol engine (140 bhp at 4,500 rpm) or the, now more familiar, 6-cylinder 4-litre diesel. In 1984 the 70 Series, short wheelbase Land Cruiser 2 arrived in the UK. As was by now normal practice, only a limited specification was imported. In fact only one model was available, a two-door diesel-driven station wagon. By the end of the decade the Prado, as it was known outside the UK, was revamped with new engines and styles. However, 1990 began with the importation of the highest specification ever for a Toyota with the development of the luxurious 80 Series. The VX Land Cruiser had arrived to meet the Range Rover head on.

Despite the huge bulk, over 1.85 metres wide and 4.8 metres long, the VX Land Cruiser is amazingly supple over extremes of terrain. On both the front and rear it has live axles with trailing arms, Panhard rod, coil springs and anti-roll bars. ABS is standard to the servo-assisted dual-circuit ventilated disc brakes. Unlike the Range Rover, it has retained the handbrake on rear drums rather than using a transmission brake. The all-new 6-cylinder 4164 cc OHC, direct injection diesel engine is turbocharged and intercooled to produce a growling 165 bhp at 3,600 rpm and 265 lb/ft at 1,800 rpm. The electronically-controlled automatic gearbox (few manual models have been imported to the UK) has permanent FWD with a viscous-controlled centre differential. It also has diff. locks on the axles. The departure angle is affected by the spare wheel which is attached on the underside of the rear body. The VX will safely tow 3,500kg.

The Toyota HiLux Pickup has been a popular 4x4 for more than a decade, both with people requiring its large carrying capacity and those who just want an impressive-looking off roader. Currently the single cab is the only model imported to the UK by Toyota, although the sensible twin-cab is popular elsewhere, but only available in the UK as a special import. The engine choice is either a modest 2.5-litre diesel producing 81 bhp at 4,200 rpm and 121 lb/ft at 2,400 rpm or the 2.2-litre petrol giving 92 bhp at 4,400 rpm.

Secondhand Toyota Land Cruisers

The Land Cruiser range imported during the 1980s has very different short and long wheelbase versions, the latter being 187-in. It has a poor ramp-breakover-angle, like the Nissan Patrol. The Land Cruiser GX is a five-door utility estate with the possibility of being a seven-seater. It has part-time FWD and was originally sold with the 3980 cc diesel engine (102 bhp at 3,500 rpm, 171 lb/ft at 1,800 rpm) as standard. By the late 1980s this had been replaced by the all new

165 bhp 4164 cc diesel engine. Suspension is of the more old-fashioned leaf springs and live axles, although some later models did have coil sprung suspension and differential locks. Towing maximum is 3,500 kg.

The Land Cruiser 2 (as it was known in the UK) is a three-door station wagon and began arriving in Europe around the mid-1980s. A short wheelbase vehicle, it has part-time FWD and is powered by a 2446 cc diesel turbo OHC engine with 84 bhp at 4,000 rpm and 138 lb/ft at 2,400 rpm. This has live axles but coil springs. There is a limited slip differential fitted as standard. It can tow up to 2,000 kg.

UMM

Originally designed and built in France, the Alter model now comes from Portugal. There are few vehicles on the secondhand market in the UK and most of the early ones were personal imports. These vehicles had a Peugeot 2304 cc diesel engine (67 bhp at 4,500 rpm, 134 lb/ft at 2,200 rpm). Since the importers SMC Industrial took over the UK franchise this rugged off-roader has steadily made strong headway on to the scene as a utility vehicle, competing strongly with the Land Rover. The Alter 11 covers a wide range of variants in both a short wheelbase (100-in) and long wheelbase (121-in) form. These exist as soft tops, hard tops, pickups, flat beds, tippers and station wagons. The five-door model of the latter is a comfortable twelve-seater. All are driven by the well tried and tested Peugeot 4-cylinder diesel engine. The naturally-aspirated form produces 76 bhp at 4,500 rpm, whilst the other option is the intercooled, turbocharged diesel that gives out 110 bhp at 4,150 rpm. Transmission of these vehicles has part-time FWD and is capable of towing 3,500 kg on a braked trailer. Parts are easy to obtain including the GKN axles.

Illustrations, facing page:
Top: *Fig. 2.27   UMM hardtop, SWB, trialling*
Centre: *Fig. 2.28   Vauxhall Frontera Sport at an AWDC meeting (Courtesy of Vauxhall Motors)*
Bottom: *Fig. 2.29   Pinzgauer Turbo D (Courtesy of Overland Ltd)*

VAUXHALL

This British subsidiary of General Motors recently entered the leisure market with the Frontera models which had elsewhere in the world been available under the Isuzu badge with various names such as Mu, Rodeo and Amigo. The short wheelbase (94-in), three-door model wears the Sport badge and features a 2-litre petrol engine that produces 110 bhp at 5,200 rpm and 125 lb/ft at 2,600 rpm. The long wheelbase (110-in), five-door estate has two engine options: the 2.4-litre petrol engine, like the Sport, has multi-point fuel injection, and produces 120 bhp at 4,800 rpm and 144 lb/ft torque at 2,200 rpm. The 2.3-litre, turbocharged diesel is intercooled to produce 96 bhp at 4,200 rpm and 159 lb/ft of torque at 2,200 rpm. Four-wheel drive is part-time.

The front suspension consists of independent double wishbones with torsion bar springs and anti-roll bar, whilst the rear has a live axle on semi-elliptic leaf springs. It can tow a braked trailer weight of 2,000 kg.

Vauxhall has been the first 4x4 manufacturer to give private customers a chance of an off-road driving course as part of the package when buying a new vehicle.

OTHER COMMERCIALS

Of the top commercial vehicles suited to off roading and expedition work, two stand out: the Mercedes Unimog and the Pinzgauer from Steyr-Daimler-Puch. Both are very expensive but are high quality machines.

The Austrian built Pinzgauer is available with its straight 6-six cylinder 2383cc, turbocharged diesel (from Volkswagen), as either 4x4 or 6x6. Although it is a monster of a machine, even the 6x6 has an incredible off-road capacity. It has around thirteen inches of ground clearance, an impressive axle articulation that is amazingly supple and sets of differential locks. Approach and departure angles are more than acceptable at 40 and 45 degrees respectively. An automatic ZF transmission is available with the turbo D engine. This produces 105 bhp at 4,350 rpm and torque of 158 lb/ft at 2,800 rpm. It has very good loading capacity. The five-seater, 716 model is a 4x4, whilst the 718 is a 6x6. The former, 96-in wheelbase, can carry a 1,250 kg payload whilst the 718 model can take up to 1,700 kg. The independent suspension of both has swing half axles in a portal axle design. This provides for the good ground clearance. Body styles are complemented by a number of campervan/motorhome variants which make this a superb way of exploring the world. It provides an unbelievably capable, yet reliable and manageable, machine which is still containerisable. The build quality is high, utilising many interior parts from Mercedes G-wagen.

In many ways the Pinzgauer vehicles are the Rolls Royce of off-road machines. Built and developed by Steyr-Daimler-Puch over many years, these are expensive but formidable all-terrain off-roaders.

The Mercedes Unimog is a very impressive concept machine. It has been around for several decades building up a formidable reputation as a rugged all-wheel drive system. Although very expensive Unimogs can be found working in many countries of the world. They are available in compact form or heavy duty long wheelbase format. The latest models have three independently acting drive systems: power-take-offs, special drives and hydraulic systems. One drive concept even allows for a conversion to rail operation so that it can pull up to 600 tonnes of rolling stock. The permanent FWD also has axle diff. locks. Portal axles provide excellent ground clearance and yet a low centre of gravity. The sophisticated drive system even allows for reverse in all gears. The 6-cylinder diesel engine produces 102 bhp at 2,400 rpm for the non-turbo version or 156 bhp for the top specification. The body and implement formats are so numerous that you wonder if they can think up any more variations!

Yet another commercial vehicle developed and built in Germany is the Volkswagen Tristar. Based on the synchro-equipped Transporter chassis the Tristar is an adaptable twin-crew cab pickup with a smooth 2109 cc water-cooled, 4-cylinder petrol injection engine. This produces 112 bhp at 4,800 rpm and 128 lb/ft at 2,800 rpm. A 70 bhp 1588 cc turbo-diesel is also available but tends to be underpowered for this body. The suspension consists of double wishbones and coil springs with track arm, anti-roll bar and hydraulic dampers at the front. Drive to the front wheels is permanently engaged via a viscous transmission unit so that torque is only transmitted to the front wheels when slip is detected on the rear axle. This is gradually applied, but if the land is considered difficult then the driver can engage the differential locks for both front and rear axles. Ground clearance is rather limited, but this is an accomplished and beautifully made machine.

The 2-tonne HUGO 8x8 is somewhat of a specialist off-road vehicle which has been developed in the UK and is now manufactured by MWG All Terrain Vehicles Ltd. The vehicle is a versatile load carrier, capable of taking personnel or payload over heavy terrain that might leave other off roaders struggling. A hefty 4-litre Perkins Phaser 110T turbocharged diesel powers the HUGO (High Utility Global Operations) which drives through a three-speed automatic transmission.

ENGINE CONVERSIONS

The 4x4 is a versatile beast, not least because of the large space under the bonnet, but four-wheel drive enthusiasts often have good reasons for wanting to change its heart. They aim for two extremes: they want either more power and torque or to remove a thirsty petrol engine in favour of diesel unit.

The advantages and disadvantages of the two fuels are further discussed in the chapter on expeditions as the change is not just for fuel economy or power. A conversion is best carried out by one of

Fig. 2.30 Nissan 3.5 -litre Turbo Intercooled engine conversion in a Range Rover

the many companies which specialise in the craft. (See Useful Addresses.) Changing an engine is not just a simple case of undoing the engine mounts and disconnecting it from the gearbox, even if it is the same type of unit. One of the simplest forms of conversion is to change fuel types using the vehicle manufacturer's standard engines. The Land Rover, from the earliest version, is one of the most converted vehicles to be found. The switch between the basic petrol and diesel 2.25-litre engine is very straightforward as they were developed using the same engine block. No alteration is necessary to the engine bay or gearbox. There are slight differences in the exhaust system but once the engines have been swopped the only major reorganisation is in the fuel lines and electrics. In the more complex conversions, these are the aspects that cause most of the problems to the transplant. The cost of a good carburetted Rover V8 is so low that there is quite a trend amongst many mud-plugging off roaders to fit these engines to Series One or Two Land Rovers. Although relatively easy the conversion requires a modification to the bulkhead to accommodate the new size. Considerable thought is then required over the gearbox. Due to the power passing through the transmission it may be prudent to consider a reconditioned Range Rover gearbox.

To help the home enthusiast there are companies that specialise in producing conversion kits for most types of engines and 4x4s. The prime part, machined for the job, is an adapter plate that is necessary to couple the foreign engine to the existing gearbox. Changes may also be necessary to the chassis so that the engine can be bolted on to new mounts. The sight, not to mention the sound, of a high compression V8 in a Series One is impressive although a sudden surge of new power may cause problems with differentials and brakes. Needless to say, an upgrade in tyres is of paramount importance if the new machine is to bowl down the motorway at the legal speed limit.

Today's diesels are a world apart from the agricultural units of the 1960s and 1970s. At that time petrol engines were in favour because of their increased power when fuel was cheap. The story is now very different. Diesel is cheaper and produces more MPG. Thirsty luxury vehicles which have been in production long enough to produce a good secondhand market, such as the Range Rover, are the prime subjects for conversion.

Considerations for changing to Diesel

Fuel costs:
Most diesel engines use at least a third less fuel than petrol versions. When travelling outside the UK there is a significant price differential: diesel can be half the price of petrol. Improved fuel consumption therefore increases the range of the fuel tank: ideal for travel and expedition use.

Torque:
Because of the diesel engines ability to operate at higher temperatures than a petrol engine it produces more torque as well as being more efficient. The higher torque provides a better pull, and therefore yields an improved towing ability.

Pollution:
As diesel engines are more efficient, they produce fewer pollution-causing emissions.

Other operating costs:
Servicing costs are significantly lower with a diesel engine, mainly due to the lack of electrics. Diesel engines, properly cared for, can be more reliable and give a longer life expectancy than a petrol unit.

Appreciation:
A new engine is like a heart transplant and will significantly increase the longevity of the vehicle. With today's modern diesel engine and the demand for diesel-driven vehicles there is a higher resale value than a petrol one.

Safety:
Diesel is far less hazardous than petrol where fire is concerned. When travelling abroad and on expeditions this would be an important consideration, particularly when using jerrycans.

Future costs:
Professionals converting engines can replace many deteriorating parts such as suspension, exhaust, battery and radiator. By gauging the time just right for a conversion you can cut down on expenditure in the future.

If you want a diesel 4x4 then why not buy one instead of converting? This relates to availability. Very few diesel vehicles were produced because the original market was small; therefore they are scarce and even more difficult to find in a 'non-workhorse' trim. In addition, you can specify the choice of power unit and know the history. Turbochargers are expensive items to replace if the engine is not correctly serviced. This is why many people see a better investment in purchasing a clean secondhand vehicle with high Vogue specification and good transmission and fit a brand-new diesel engine. The financial savings may not always be immediate and it can be a difficult decision to know which engine to buy. There is a plethora of engines on the market, both new and secondhand, ranging in price up to a cool £7,000 and more.

Which engine option is just one aspect to consider. The companies and agents that supply the conversion also provide a suitable installation, the intention of which is to produce a finished product to look as though it should be there and not an afterthought. Specially manufactured exhaust systems may be required as well as modification to the cooling system although most installations tend towards using off-the-shelf parts. This also refers to ancillary equipment for switching a diesel engine on and off.

Turbocharging is commonplace on today's modern diesel engines but is not necessarily that efficient. The energy produced by these engines depends on the difference in temperature between the input gas mixture and the exhaust output. The cooler the input the better the efficiency. The effect of the turbocharger is to ram air into the engine, increasing the available oxygen and thus increasing the power. The charger is driven by the exhaust gases on emission from the engine and the more rapid the engine burn the hotter the air in the turbocharger becomes. The result of this is a physical transfer of heat from the exhaust to the turbocharger. On the one hand, more air is being rammed into the engine to produce more torque but, on the other, the air is expanding under the high temperature of the hard-working engine. The principle of intercooling is to reduce the temperature of the turbocharger. This reduction in temperature ensures that the cooler air that is rammed into the engine is more dense, thus increasing the amount of oxygen in the mixture and producing a greater efficiency of burn. This should, therefore, increase the torque and bhp of the engine. Fuel consumption tends to remain the same. The most noticeable effect of intercooling is the reduction in engine noise, especially from the turbo, which can sound like a very active dentist drill!

See Useful Addresses for conversions; many of these have agents around the UK.

Engine options for the Range Rover/Land Rover

Land Rover	VM 2.5 turbo	119 bhp
Land Rover	200 TDi	111 bhp
BMW (Series M2)	2.5 turbo (6 cylinder)	115 bhp
Daihatsu	2.8 DTi	101 bhp
Isuzu	2.8 turbo/intercooled	95 & 120 bhp
Mazda	3.5 nat. aspirated	99 bhp
	3.5 turbo	120 bhp
	3.5 turbo intercooled	135 bhp
Mercedes	3.0 turbo	113 bhp
Nissan	3.5 nat. aspirated	104 bhp
	3.5 turbo	130 bhp
	3.5 turbo intercooled	148 bhp
Perkins/Mazda (4.182)	3.0 nat. aspirated	85 bhp
	3.0 turbo	100 bhp
	3.0 turbo waste-gated	108 bhp

ENVIRONMENTAL NOTE

Some of the vehicles mentioned in this chapter will run on unleaded petrol. Check with the manufacturers to see if your vehicle is capable of using 'green fuel'. Others, like early Land Rovers, can be converted to run on this fuel. Hardened valve seats are essential and exchange cylinder heads are available from a number of manufacturers. An alternative is to use a fuel additive such as PowerPlus. Also on the market are an increasing number of various 'fuel saving' devices. Many of these use some form of magnet on the fuel line to 'rearrange' the fuel molecules.

3

Vehicle Preparation

INTRODUCTION

Driving off road will put a strain on your vehicle never experienced on road. It is noteworthy that a FWD vehicle not driven off road usually maintains a higher resale value. An incident in the New Forest some years ago illustrates the importance some drivers attach to this. Tall gorse bushes hemmed in the muddy track but suddenly, up ahead, the reversing lights of a vehicle appeared through the thickening undergrowth. 'A bit scratchy', commented the driver, who obviously preferred to reverse through glutinous mud and risk getting stuck than scratch his paintwork!

Scratched paintwork and small dents are the almost inevitable trademarks of off roading. However, expect the worst and try to give some protection to the vehicle. First of all: make sure that your vehicle is in a roadworthy condition, as the manufacturer intended. Remove any lights (e.g. fog lights) that may have been fitted below the bumper, because you can guarantee they will not last very long. Registration plates should be on the bodywork or above the bumper. It is worth investing in a set of pressed aluminium plates. Fitted correctly, they will last, although the figures may need to be repainted occasionally with matt black paint.

Check the following on your vehicle as off roading increases the chances of their breakdown and the failure of any of them off road could be dangerous.

- steering joints
- brakes and brake pipes
- exhaust system - check for areas where it sounds like blowing, particularly when it attaches to the manifold. This is the commonest area for faults after driving off road
- springs and bushes
- fuel tank, principally check the base for dents and possible leaks

- lights and wiring are in good order; poor clips and loose connections easily shake loose. This includes the clamping for the battery
- tighten all fittings if loose, e.g. door handles, spare wheel, roof rack - in fact anything that might shake loose off road

Preparations for off roading will inevitably vary according to the expected terrain and duration of the trip. Whenever possible, go with another 4x4 vehicle: if (when!) you become stuck or break down there will be help available to tow you. However, help from your colleague is only going to be forthcoming if you maintain a good space between the two vehicles. Always cross mires, deep stretches of mud or climb steep hills one at a time, i.e. one vehicle should be kept on firm ground to help the other. On hills it is more a case of safety. Remember that braking distances are extended due to possible damp brakes or steepness. Keep a wide margin of error between vehicles. The driver of the second vehicle can also make a careful note of how the first driver tackles obstacles, looking for difficult spots and alternatives. CB radio is a cheap and useful way of keeping in contact. It saves considerable time jumping in and out of vehicles and a sore throat from shouting across mud and rivers.

OUTSIDE THE VEHICLE

Protrusions
If you have manual freewheeling hubs fitted, make sure they are engaged well before you start off roading. If you have differential locks make sure you lock them in plenty of time and well before the wheels begin to spin. Mirrors should be turned inwards as they will be the first thing to catch on hedges and banks, and are costly to replace. If they are mounted on the wing and are not flip-back types they will not only regularly break but also cause dents in the wing. After several years they can cause substantial wing damage. A tow hitch can also cause damage to the vehicle when off road. If it hangs particularly low on the vehicle it can easily catch on rocks and tree stumps. What is important is to be aware of the presence of this low tow hitch and to drive accordingly (see Fig. 3.1). It is not unknown for the rear cross-member of a Land Rover to be ripped off by the tow hitch.

Fig. 3.1 Hung up on the rear tow hitch, this Suzuki cannot get traction with the rear wheels

Vision and spare wheels

Due to the large sizes of off-road wheels, spares are often carried on the outside of the vehicle. Recently-manufactured vehicles tend to have strengthened rear doors on which to hang the spare wheel. The bonnet is a common area to use, especially for Land Rovers. The reduction in visibility is lessened on some by fitting bonnets with a depression. If you are crossing very undulating ground, or terrain strewn with rocks and deep potholes, the reduction in visibility can become annoying and even dangerous (see Fig 3.2). Under these conditions it is preferable to have a temporary storage place either inside or on top of the vehicle (if a roof rack is fitted). Fitment to the rear door is only advisable if recommended by the manufacturer or

Fig. 3.2 Vision over the bonnet, with and without spare wheel

if the door is strengthened. Alternatively, several independent companies are marketing a spare-wheel holder that swings on a bar across the rear door (Pivlock, for example).

Rear visibility can be impaired to some degree by the presence of a spare wheel at the back. Do not be tempted to attach the wheel too low as the departure angle for the vehicle will be affected. This is a common fault on Land Rovers; a sudden, steep ascent will be followed by a broken rear door.

Aerials

These can be a problem and should be retracted. If you are using CB buy an aerial which is very flexible and has a sturdy base. If the terrain is especially bumpy the tip of the aerial can be fixed to another part of the bodywork.

Mud flaps

Very good for keeping mud and stones off bodywork and underneath especially when you are back on tarmac after off roading. However, they can get torn off when crossing deep undulating ground, particularly if you become temporarily stuck and have to reverse. During this time the flaps bend and twist, becoming trapped between the wheel and the rut and eventually becoming ripped. One solution is to use rubber 'bungies' (elasticated luggage straps) to hold them in position so that whilst reversing the 'spring loading' prevents them from going forward. It may be necessary to punch a small hole in the flap into which the hook of one end of the bungie can be inserted then the other end clipped onto the grab handle of a Land Rover (or rear bumper on other vehicles).

Lights

Driving off road at night is a fascinating experience. Even when it is a track, or terrain that you know well, in the dark it takes on a very different dimension. The design of off-road vehicles, especially the older Land Rovers, left much to be desired when it came to lighting the road.

One of the first things to do is check the state of the reflectors. Off roading does cause damage to these, especially the ones attached to the edge of the bodywork. Bulbs have a tendency to dim with age and may need renewing before they cease functioning. Having satisfied yourself that the existing lights are serviceable it might be worth considering auxiliary lighting. This is essential if you are likely to go off road at night as it reduces the fatigue and eye-strain that is otherwise inevitable. The shadows created by two standard headlights when crossing rough terrain call for tremendous concentration from the driver to distinguish the difference between a simple depression or an axle-bending hazard.

The fitting of additional lighting, such as spots or driving lights, must be wired in accordance with the law of the country in question. This should be checked when the lights are purchased. Make sure your wiring and battery is up to scratch. For example, the current needed for some lights may require relays to be fitted to save burning out the switch and wires.

Think sensibly about the position of the extra lights. Do not fit them under the bumper as they will be ripped off the first time you go off road. When fitting them above the bumper try to locate them as far back as possible so that anything touching the bumper will not break the lights. The siting of two large spot lights in front of the radiator can restrict air flow through the cooling system. This is a particular problem with Land Rover Turbo Diesels when travelling in hot climates. One can find a problem with most locations for auxiliary lights but one of the better places is above the windscreen, especially if you have a substantial roof rack to which you can attach them. If not, a bar can be fitted across the top of the vehicle. It is illegal, when the vehicle is used on road, to have lights positioned up high and badly adjusted.

When driving at night, as well as using the standard vehicle lights, spots at the bumper level should be angled to face up in the air whilst those at roof level should face downwards. Keep covers over the light lenses when on the road. Some more expensive lights have wire grill stone guards to protect them off road. A work light (sometimes referred to as a ploughing light) is very useful on the rear of the vehicle for reversing, loading or even pitching a tent in the dark. Make sure you have an illuminated switch or warning light to tell you when it is operating as it must not be used when driving forward.

Protection and skidplates

A number of modern off-road vehicles come with skidplates fitted as standard. This is due to the vulnerability of certain components. These plates are heavy-duty steel and can be purchased for most Japanese and American vehicles (although only from the United States). When using extreme ramp breakover angle a simple centre skidplate can be constructed from 4 mm mild steelplate. Alternatively, heavy gauge aluminium could be used. This is bolted to the gearbox cross-members and will act like a sledge to save these from digging into the ground. The 90 and 110 Land Rovers have relatively vulnerable front steering. It is wise to check on the earlier models that the later track-rod catcher plate is fitted. If not, we strongly recommend that you fit one. They are not expensive and only take half an hour to fit to the underside of the front diff. Failure to do so will result in a bent track-rod on even mild off roading.

A Devon firm, Southdown Engineering, manufacture a very good range of steering, underbody, and fuel tank protection plates as supplied to the MOD (see Fig. 3.3).

Plastic protectors

In recent years more 4x4 manufacturers are fitting more plastic protection to the lower half of the vehicle, reducing the effect of stones and vegetation. It is also possible to buy various forms of plastic protectors both for the side panels and the vulnerable lighting at the front and rear. EGR Plastics produce robust acrylic pads to protect headlamps on and off the road. Fitted in seconds, without the need for tools, it cannot be removed unless the bonnet is up. It is, therefore, theft proof.

Fig. 3.3 Practical underbody protection by Southdown Engineering

INSIDE THE VEHICLE

Loose articles, flying through the air inside the vehicle, can be distracting, annoying and dangerous. Try to ensure that items such as cassettes, jacks and aerosol cans are stowed away carefully. If they are loose, not only will they hit people, particularly on head and legs, but they may end up under the accelerator and brake pedals. Large articles in the back of the vehicle can be strapped down with bungies, taped into place or secured by spring-clips. After a while it becomes second nature to find a home for potentially loose articles.

Off-road vehicles normally have battery-holding brackets fitted as standard but it is worth checking that these are working and are on tight. After being serviced in garages this is not always the case.

Steering wheel

When driving on uneven ground the steering will constantly flick from side to side. Develop a habit never to put your thumbs inside the steering wheel - sudden kick-back will bruise if not break them. Power steering will reduce but not eliminate the possibility. The latest problem that can happen is due to a soft covered steering wheel: if your thumbs are through the spokes, a kick of the wheel, and your thumb nial can dig in. This results in a painfully ripped nail. Keep your thumbs up at all times!

On the subject of power steering, it does reduce the 'feel' for the terrain that you are on. Although this does mean that with power steering it is possible to be quick to manoeuvre, there is a danger that one will over-correct when travelling down gullies and deep, rutted tracks. Concentration must be quite intense under these conditions in order to prevent the vehicle going out of control when driving with power steering. Perhaps one of the slight disadvantages of power steering whilst off road is the loss of 'feel' for front wheel direction. You could be slipping straight and be on full lock but not realise this. Do not be afraid to poke your head out the window to check.

TYRES

Whatever vehicle you have, the performance of it will ultimately be down to the ability, or otherwise, of the tyres to grip the ground and to perform well in the terrain you are trying to cross. There is not a tyre made that is perfect for all conditions; the advice we give is based on personal experience and the collected views of 4x4 off-road drivers from around the world, rather than the findings of scientific research. Thus it is offered to you in that spirit. For this reason we cannot be held responsible for any events or circumstances arising from the use or misuse of this information.

When considering what tyres to use there are first of all two questions to ask yourself.

What can you afford?

What is most practical for your use?

The two basic forms of tyre are cross-ply and radial. In recent years the former tyre has lost some favour and may be associated with cheapness. This may be so but in the off-road market there are a number of excellent off-road cross-ply tyres giving a wide selection of possible tread patterns. Radial tyres are more expensive but last longer than cross-ply. Radials have a lower rolling resistance. This yields an improved fuel economy as well as reduced wear and tear. In addition, they produce a softer ride and better road holding, especially when hitting bumps in tarmac roads. Most Japanese and American 4x4s have 15-in wheels as standard. Your choice of tyres may, therefore, be restricted to American ones unless you change to different size rims. Vehicles with 16-in wheels have a much wider range of tyres and tread patterns available. This diversity increases still further with the introduction of new tyres from the United States.

Very wide tyres have increased street credibility but decreased ability to cope with wet conditions. On wet grass they have a tendency to float, thus reducing traction. A narrower tyre will cut through the water and bite on to the surface increasing the traction. This flotation effect of wide tyres can be put to advantage on very soft sand (on dunes for example), but overall may cause more problems (where do you store the spare wheel?)

Vehicle performance over cross-country routes will be influenced by the degree of ground contact, either by the tyre grip to the ground or the tyres' ability to 'float' over the terrain. The problem of tyre choice is that different terrains require differing widths and tread patterns.

A tyre for crossing sand will have to be wide, low pressured (to increase the surface area at the bottom of the tyre) and have a tread that will not cut the top layer of ground. True sand tyres have virtually no tread. The balloon types one sees in the ergs (thousands of square miles of 'Beau Geste' sand dunes) of the Sahara are

Fig. 3.4 Michelin XCL

Fig. 3.5 Firestone SAT (Super All Traction

Fig. 3.6 Goodyear High-Miler

Fig. 3.7 Goodyear Wrangler

Fig. 3.8 Michelin XZY

Fig. 3.9 Goodyear S&G

capable of taking a heavy vehicle up the side of steep dunes. Once off sandy ground they can be dangerous and are downright lethal on wet Tarmac.

The requirements for mud and wet grass are very different to sand. The tyre must be thin with an aggressive tread to cut through the upper layers of ground. The tread should be able to shed its load of mud and sediment as quickly as it collects. A clogged tread is totally useless and will just spin round, having dug your vehicle into the mire. Therefore, a tread may not be as effective as it looks. Find out if it has the ability to self-clean before you buy it.

For most people, off roading represents a very small proportion of their total mileage - over 90 per cent will be on paved road. An off road, aggressive tread will wear quickly if used mainly on the road and will not have such good manners as a normal road tyre. It will also tend to be noisy. The town and country tread of the Goodyear High-Miler was used extensively by the army on their Series Three Land Rovers. You could hear an army convoy driving along a road several miles away!

One compromise on tyres is to have two sets, an on-road Michelin radial set which can last over 50,000 miles and an off-road cross-ply set with an aggressive tread pattern. This is convenient only if your off roading comes in blocks between long periods of road driving, but it can make the latter more comfortable. It is also a very economic compromise once the initial outlay has been made.

Buying part-worn or retread tyres is another way of keeping cost down. Modern retreads are made to a high specification and are excellent value for money. Two very good off-road tyres sold by Ponthir Tyre Services are the Mud Plugger X-ply with a SAT tread and the Tracker with an MT tread, which is a radial remould. Re-cut tyres are illegal on a Land Rover and would nullify the insurance. Part-worns are an excellent way to save money when purchasing normally expensive tyres. The Ministry of Defence sell large numbers of tyres to various outlets, for example those companies dealing in ex-military vehicles.

Check the Yellow Pages for possible local outlets. (See also Useful Addresses.) When buying secondhand tyres check that their walls are in good condition, both inside and out if possible.

Most cross-ply tyres have a ply rating of around 6. This is a measure of the wall strength. If your vehicle is likely to carry much weight and travel over hard uneven ground you may consider a higher rating of 8. Michelin XYZ tyres owe much of their longevity to the 12-ply rating. The drawback with a tyre of this strength is the difficulty experienced in taking it on and off the rims. Some tyre fitting companies are not equipped to do this.

When driving on the road it is essential for safety and economy to maintain the correct air pressures in the tyres as recommended by the manufacturer. Off road it may be necessary to change these pressures.

Consequently it can be easy to forget and drive on roads with under-inflated tyres. This can be very dangerous and the extra heat generated can cause excessive wear, ultimately causing premature failure.

When the going is soft off road it can help, in an emergency, to drop the tyre pressures. Most 4x4 vehicle handbooks will tell you how low you can afford to go. As a rough guide for an unladen short wheelbase vehicle the pressure can be reduced to 18 psi for the front and 20 psi in the rear. Long wheelbase vehicles, with the heavier weight, need more in the rear tyres, approximately 24 psi. Remember to keep your speed down below 25 mph as wall damage is a problem with soft tyres. Don't forget that ground clearance is reduced with lower tyre pressures. So, for a variety of reasons, reinflate tyres as soon as possible. This will inevitably mean that you need to carry a pump in the vehicle with an accurate pressure gauge. The following are possible alternatives to the traditional, slow foot pump:

1. Mini Electric Air Compressor: several are on the market from car accessory shops and they can be plugged into cigarette lighter sockets or connected directly to the battery. Do not rely on the pressure gauge which is usually attached to the pump.
2. Carbon Dioxide Cylinders: a simple attachment allows a rapid inflation with carbon dioxide. Some double up as fire extinguishers.
3. If you have ARB Air Lockers then the air compressor fitted into their system can be used very effectively.

An additional and essential item is a separate pressure gauge. By having it clipped to the dashboard it can be found quickly and will be prevented from rolling around.

Ideally, tyre pressures should be taken when the tyre is cold. After a run on Tarmac or if the climate is hot the air inside the tyre soon heats up and increases the pressure. Around the Mediterranean on a summer's afternoon you can expect tyre pressures to have doubled. Be aware of the changes that occur in your tyres under differing conditions as this will minimise any problems that you are likely to encounter. Carbon dioxide in the tyre does not exert the same pressure changes with increased heat as air. Nitrogen produces a minimal change with temperature. Some expeditions setting off for the Sahara inflated their tyres with nitrogen before setting out, but there may be a problem later on if pressure changes are required!

It is very difficult to advise precisely what tyres to buy for your off-road vehicle as this is closely determined by the conditions you will be encountering. The following list is a guide to the tyres that will suit the different terrains you are most likely to come across.

Tyres for 16-in rims
Armstrong MET crossply is a good dual-purpose tyre. Although effective in mud it can become clogged quite quickly. The Avon

Fig. 3.10 BF Goodrich Radial All-Terrain T/A

Rangemaster and Pirelli LR04 radial-ply are long-tasting tyres suitable for an overland trek where a reasonable performance both on and off road is required. Firestone SAT cross-ply stands for Super All-Traction and it does just that. Often considered the poor man's off-road tyre it gives excellent grip in heavy off-road conditions. The Firestone Town and Country tread is not quite as aggressive but is marginally cheaper and quieter on road. The Goodyear All-Service Bar Tread cross-ply has been fitted to all military vehicles since the year dot. A very good dual-purpose and long-tasting tyre. Mickey Thompson radial tyres are wide and very aggressive off road but have good on-road manners. They give excellent grip in all situations but are not cheap.

Michelin radial-ply tyres are available in a wide range of treads. The XM treads have excellent on-road manners. The XCL, as used by the military, has good mud-gripping qualities but limited sideways stability. The XS tread pattern is best suited to sand and not so good in mud, as the tread is quite capable off road considering that it is not aggressive. It is very strong and really does last. A good expedition tyre, it copes well with sand and rocky terrain.

Tyres for 15-in rims

Armstrong produce a range of tyres. The Norseman is a general purpose tyre which is very good on road, especially in snow, and has a reasonable performance off road. The Mud Track Armstrong is more of an off-road tyre and behaves in a similar manner to the BF Goodrich MT and General Grabber MT. Both of these are biased towards off-road use. They are wide and therefore give good flotation on sand. In slippery situations, e.g. wet grass, they are more likely to lose traction. The Grabber tread tends to self-clean better than the Mud Track and the BF and is also a cheaper buy. Yokohama Mud Digger tyres are quite new to the United Kingdom and need to prove their off-road capability. In the meantime they appear to perform in an impressive way under heavy off-road conditions and their on-road manners seem surprisingly good for a tyre with such aggressive tread.

Tyre Wear

Check tyres regularly for cuts and abrasions, particularly on the wall. Keep pressures up to the manufacturer's recommended level when on road. Chemical compounds can be injected into the tyre air space which will give a certain degree of immunity to punctures, e.g. Tyrerite.

WATERPROOFING

Although one can go to considerable expense to waterproof an engine completely (necessary only for long periods of total immersion), the general off-roader will still benefit from keeping water out. It is a good idea to minimise the chances of water entering

Fig. 3.11 Simple wading precautions should be taken in situations like this

the electrics even when on road, and with the knowledge of possible wading ahead a few precautions are essential:

- See that the coil is positioned as high as possible in the engine compartment
- Always carry silicone grease in your tool box. Wipe a small quantity round the distributor cap: a) where the leads enter and b) around the cap base to form a seal
- A silicone spray also helps. Spray across the plugs, coil and distributor before entering water. An oil spray such as WD40 also helps to disperse water after wading, when the engine refuses to turn over correctly as it is only firing on half the cylinders! In an emergency some hair sprays will work as long as they are used prior to wading. The principle is just to produce some form of seal over the electrics to repel water.
- Rubber waterproof covers can be purchased for some makes of distributor but a cheap and effective alternative is to use a rubber glove stretched over the cap. Cling film, too, can make a temporary shield to cover electrical components. Perhaps the most effective method consists of a plastic drink bottle which can be cut to fit the distributor and shield the component from at least 80% of water and mud. (See Fig. 3.12.)

V8 engines are especially prone to water-on-electrics problems as the distributor is adjacent to the fan, which succeeds in dumping water right on top of it. A simple shield for this can be made from thin gauge aluminium sheet. Separating the distributor from the fan spray, it should be angled over the top, towards the engine, to protect against water dripping from the bonnet. Also make sure that if the air intake is facing towards the fan a suitable aluminium sheet is constructed which will shield it but not restrict the air flow.

Diesel engines, with their lack of electrics, suffer little from water contamination and therefore need minimal waterproofing. If water enters the fuel system, however, serious problems can occur. Wading in water deeper than 50 cm may cause water to drip into the air filter. Under these conditions a raised air intake should be considered. Aquasolve is a fuel additive produced by Thermo-Fluids Engineering Research Centre at City University, London, and marketed by Shurflo Ltd. It can be added to any water-contaminated diesel and cause it to be bonded or absorbed. In this way it can be

Fig. 3.12   Simple distributor protection – a cut-out drinks bottle

burnt along with the rest of the DERV. It is said to improve the combustion, clean the system of micro-organisms and increase the life of the injector system. It could be useful on expeditions and it also works with seawater. It is expensive and the common alternative would be to fit an extra, in-line paper fuel filter element.

Many types of vehicles have had extension pipes fitted to the exhaust system, used for wading rivers. This is really unnecessary. We ourselves had vehicles that have stopped in deep water and then have restarted after a period of time.

A large fertiliser bag or a plastic/polythene dustbin liner can be quite effective in reducing water intake to the engine compartment over the top of the radiator. Secure it in place with the bonnet, with the liner on the outside of the radiator. If water does get in, the radiator fan will spray it around the engine. If you regularly enter water you might consider buying an electric fan (Kenlowe make one - see Useful Addresses), and fit it with an override switch so that it can be stopped prior to wading. They are said to reduce fuel consumption.

Wading plugs and axle breathers

Not all vehicles have them, so you will need to consult the relevant manufacturer's handbook. They are fitted before wading in deep water. The plug is threaded at one end whilst the other is square sectioned enabling it to be gripped with a socket or spanner. They fit into the bell housing, and some timing belt covers, to stop the ingress of mud and water through the breather hole. Make sure that the axle breathers are not clogged with mud or covered by rust.

They have two important functions. First, they maintain an equal pressure inside and outside the axle casing. If they are blocked, an internal pressure builds and then oil will be blown past the oil seals. Second, when working as a valve, they will prevent the entry of water and mud. Modern Land Rovers use an extended breather. Older vehicles can be converted by fitting a long polythene pipe which stands up higher than any likely water level - a cheap but effective means of protection.

Bushes

The modern 4x4 coil suspension is an excellent form of springing. It is softer and gives more axle travel than a leaf sprung vehicle. However, the axles need locating to the chassis with strong longitudinal arms. Rubber bushing is needed to give flexibility where they pivot. Extreme axle travel and abrasion whilst off road will cause rapid wear. Bushes should therefore be checked for such wear on a regular basis, especially the front Panhard Rod. Wear will cause the vehicle to become unstable. If you use your vehicle regularly off road it would be a good precautionary measure to have a second rod, pre-bushed, ready for replacement. In addition, partially worn bushes may seriously increase uneven tyre wear. A harder rubber compound bush can be obtained, the Eurathane Bush. It lasts longer, but the extra cost and loss of some flexibility may not be for you.

EQUIPMENT CHECKLIST

- can of WD40 or equivalent
- silicone grease
- large fertiliser bag or polythene/plastic dustbin liner
- wading plug if applicable
- tyre pressure gauge
- pump to reinflate tyres
- torch
- first-aid kit
- basic recovery gear - rope, shovel, high-lift jack, pair of heavy-duty gloves

PREPARATION SUMMARY

Immediately before off roading you should check that you have not forgotten any of the following points:

- travel with another vehicle whenever possible
- check vehicle is in good mechanical order
- anchor/find homes for all loose items
- be prepared for temporary waterproofing
- consider positioning of spare wheel
- consider the tow hitch
- tuck in wing mirrors and retract aerial
- check tyre pressures for suitability to terrain
- engage freewheeling hubs, if applicable
- engage FWD or differential lock
- keep those thumbs out of the steering wheel!

4

Off-Road Techniques

The main obstacles that you are most likely to encounter are dealt with in this chapter. It is inevitable that you will be confronted with combinations of these but you should practise the individual terrain tactics first. At the end of each section there is a summary of the action taken. This is for quick reference. However, *read the text first* as the summary gives just the bare essentials.

A general rule before attempting any obstacle is to check on foot, looking for those additional problems that are not obvious from behind the steering wheel. As in any driving situation, you should always be reading the conditions up ahead. Know what is 20 m in front but, more importantly, know too those few metres immediately in front of your vehicle.

There is also a tendency to drive too fast off road. This may be exhilarating but it is foolhardy. It is true that some techniques require some 'welly' to prevent getting bogged down, but there is always a chance that having got through, churning up the surface and ploughing deep ruts, your way out is blocked and you cannot return the way you came. Not only that, but this selfish attitude will make it difficult for anyone coming behind you.

Drive in haste and repent while carrying out self-recovery – you will have plenty of time!

DESCENDING SLOPES

Even a relatively simple slope off road can be tricky if the terrain is rocky or soft. But with low ratio gears slopes of one in one (i.e. 45 degrees) can be attempted. To descend such a slope may sound simple but remember the key feature is no braking. To descend in a controlled fashion necessitates first gear, low range. The torque

Fig. 4.1 Look before you leap! Always walk your route first

produced gives remarkable engine braking and needs to be felt to be believed, but make sure first gear is stable and does not jump out into neutral as this manoeuvre could then prove very dangerous.

All Rover vehicles have excellent engine braking due to the very low ratio transfer gear; their low-revving diesel engines are especially good.

Japanese off-road vehicles tend to have a higher-geared transfer box. More care should thus be exercised, particularly with the petrol models. The Suzuki has minimal engine braking in low range due to its small, high-revving engine. One trick for these vehicles, before tackling a steep descent, is to pull the handbrake on two or three notches. This slows down the transmission without locking the wheels. This strategy will of course only work with vehicles fitted with a transmission brake. Suzuki models produced in recent years have returned to the poorer system of rear drums for the handbrake. A backward step.

The golden rule is to get out and walk the slope. But what are you looking for? It is easier to go down a steep slope than it is to go up, so make sure there is a way out once you reach the bottom. This

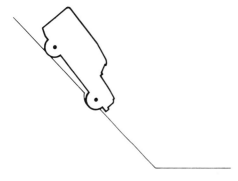

Fig. 4.2 Descending a slope. Watch out for extra depressions sending the vehicle off balance

may require a reconnoitre several hundred metres on if the terrain is obscured. As you walk down the slope look out for extra-deep holes that could make the angle of your descent too steep. If a hole is small then pick a route that straddles it. If not, look for an alternative to avoid crossing it.

Once you have decided that it is safe to drive down and you have chosen a route, check that you have engaged low range. If you have a central diff. lock ensure that this is also engaged. Select first gear in your main gearbox. Pull slowly away letting the clutch out (no riding the clutch). Kick your feet back, clear of the pedals. Under no circumstances should you attempt to apply the brakes. There is a danger that if you allow your foot to hover over the pedal the 'on road' instinct will take over and you will put your foot down hard. Braking on a steep descent will almost guarantee the wheels locking. This will lead to skidding and a faster descent. In first gear low range the descent will be controlled.

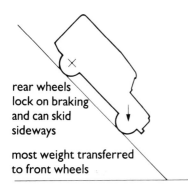

rear wheels lock on braking and can skid sideways

most weight transferred to front wheels

Fig. 4.3 When descending, weight is transferred to the front wheels, causing the rear wheels to lighten and then lock if the brakes are applied

The primary reason for not using the brakes is that braking on a steep descent transfers the vehicle's weight to the front wheels. Because little weight is on the rear wheels they lock before the front ones, and then go into a skid which tries to make the back of the vehicle travel faster than the front (see Fig. 4.3). The end result is that the vehicle pulls to one side, which can be dangerous if it gets out of control and could lead to the vehicle rolling over.

If the track is quite good and firm, so that traction can be maintained, it is possible to slow a fast descent by 'cadence braking'. This is a rhythmic pumping of the brakes, which must be done lightly enough to ensure that the wheels do not lock.

Before making any descent down a very steep slope always try to pick a line which takes a right-angled path from the top edge and then descends in a straight line. If circumstances prevent this, you had better read the section on traversing slopes – and fast!

Summary

- get out and walk it first
- wear safety belts
- select low range and lock centre diff. (if fitted)
- check first gear is engaged
- pull away – feet off all pedals
- thumbs out of steering wheel spokes
- pick a straight line down

ASCENDING SLOPES

As in the descent, walk the proposed route first. It is useless driving to the top of a slope only to discover it is impossible to get down the other side or even turn round. Again, look for your best route, watching out for extra bumps or ridges which could throw you off course and sideways on the hill. Uphill, steering becomes a problem because of the transfer of the vehicle's weight to the rear wheels, lightening the steering. If the hill is taken at speed the front wheels can leave the ground altogether! By the time the wheels touch the ground they could be half a metre to the side. With your foot still hard on the throttle you could be travelling sideways on the hill before you could do anything about it, resulting in a roll over. By walking the route first this can be avoided. You will know where

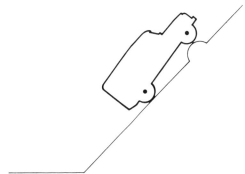

Fig. 4.4 Ascending a slope. Watch out for bumps which can launch the steering wheel, resulting in loss of control

these traps are and if they cannot be dodged all you have to do is ease off the throttle as the wheels go over the obstacles, putting your foot down hard as soon as you are past. If you do go off at an angle, don't panic but keep the power on and try to steer back on course – straight up the hill. At all costs try to keep the vehicle as perpendicular as possible to the hill, avoiding any sideways manoeuvre on the slope.

Choosing the correct gear for hill climbs becomes easier to judge with experience (see Fig. 4.5). For steep hills low range will be needed. Then select the highest gear that your engine will pull without running out of power. The lower the gear the more chance there is of wheel spin. This will usually rule out first gear, especially in those vehicles with very low ratio transfer boxes, as previously discussed under engine braking. So, second or third gear will be the likely contenders. Remember that, once you have selected a gear you will be lumbered with it. Gear changes during the ascent will be near impossible owing to the loss of vehicle momentum as soon as you depress the clutch.

One tip that may keep you going up a steep incline is to move the steering wheel quickly from side to side as you begin to lose forward motion. This helps to dig the tyres into the ground and may be enough to keep the vehicle advancing.

When you reach the top be ready to negotiate new obstacles. Your walk to the top will have told you what to expect but the bonnet could be obscuring your view. Be prepared to stop immediately the vehicle is level. If the hill goes into a rapid descent upon reaching the summit you could change down into first gear (you should already be in low range) and continue over the edge.

Summary

- walk right to the top to check the ascent and beyond
- wear seat belts
- select low range
- select suitable gear, e.g. second or third
- go up straight

DEFAULTING ON THE ASCENT

This is an important technique to practise. It should be used when you have attempted a steep ascent and then, due to either power loss and/or stalling, stopped on the slope. Again, it utilises engine braking in low range.

When forward motion on the slope ceases, put both feet on the pedals, clutch and brake. Do not use the handbrake. As quickly as possible select reverse. Check that you are in low range. If the engine is still running release both feet from the clutch and brake pedals simultaneously. Then keep them clear of the pedals so there is no temptation to brake. It is essential to come down straight – by maintaining a straight descent the engine braking will return you safely and in a controlled way to the foot of the hill. It may help to steer with one hand on top of the wheel instead of two hands as the former produces less severe movement.

If the engine is not running at the start of the descent then, simultaneously with the feet coming off the pedals, turn the ignition key to rotate the engine with the starter motor. Whether the engine starts or not, as long as it is turned over by the starter at this time it will lower you safely and gently down the hill.

Never attempt to turn round on the slope as this could cause the vehicle to roll.

If your vehicle has an automatic gearbox the same rules apply but remember that a dead engine cannot be connected through to the

Illustrations, facing page:
Fig. 4.5 Ascend in the highest gear your vehicle will pull. Watch your ramp breakover angle, stop at the top to engage lowest gear possible and descend without touching the pedals

Fig. 4.6 Defaulting on a steep hill with a soft surface. Prior correct gear selection is especially essential

wheels. In such a rare situation you must try to descend as best you can without locking the brakes and skidding out of control. If you have a transmission brake this can be pulled on two or three notches; just enough to slow the transmission but not so much that it will lock up. Failing this, a vehicle fitted with a handbrake operating rear drums will have to use cadence braking and steer straight down.

Summary

- put both feet on the pedals, clutch and brake
- do not use the handbrake
- quickly select reverse (check you are in low range)
- if engine is running:
  take both feet off clutch and brake pedals together
- if engine is not running:
  simultaneously with the feet coming off the pedals, turn the ignition key to rotate the engine
- do not brake, use engine braking only
- maintain a straight descent

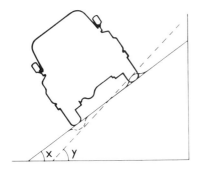

Fig. 4.7 Traversing side slopes: angle 'x' is safe under ideal conditions; angle 'y' is dangerous and can easily be caused by surface undulations

TRAVERSING SIDE SLOPES

It is best to avoid driving across a slope. If you have to do so keep your speed low and constant, checking the ground ahead. Look out for any bumps on the upper side and dips on the lower which could dramatically increase the angle. The maximum angle of tilt specified by manufacturers for their vehicles refers to controlled conditions and they do not take into consideration deviations in terrain.

Fig. 4.8 If a side slope must be traversed do so with extreme caution

Fig. 4.9 If you get into difficulties on side slopes steer down as in this instance

Whilst traversing the slope you may feel that the vehicle is about to roll. The danger here is that because the brain is on a tilt the normal reaction is to steer upwards. This will end in disastrous results! Fight this natural tendency and steer downwards.

Take into consideration any load that you may have whilst crossing a slope. A heavily-loaded roof rack will severely affect the stability. If it is not practical to get passengers out then have them shift to the high side.

Summary

- avoid driving across a slope whenever possible. If you have to:
- keep your speed low
- check ground ahead for bumps and dips
- remove any load on top of the vehicle
- eject passengers – if not possible move them to the high side

ROUGH TRACKS

Many tracks can be negotiated easily in two-wheel drive. Once the going becomes very rough or hilly use FWD but make sure you engage in plenty of time. Using FWD will reduce the strain on the transmission as well as giving extra grip.

Ruts are an inevitable problem. Try to keep the vehicle as level as possible. Driving with one set of wheels in the rut and others out will give you heavy and light wheels. The ones in the rut will have most of the vehicle's weight transferred to them and so they get the traction. This will be certain to induce wheel spin on the lighter side of the vehicle. One additional problem of this weight transfer is the increased likelihood of a puncture or tyre damage if the rutted wheel encounters a sharp rock. Fig. 4.11 shows a 12-ply tyre which blew out after such wall damage.

If you can, avoid driving in other vehicles' tracks. This may be impossible in some narrow lanes; but do not be tempted to hold the steering too tightly, the chances are the ruts will do the steering for you! It is important, however, that you know in what direction the front wheels are pointing, because a sudden increase in the lock may cause the vehicle to lurch out of the rut, producing excessive body roll and making things generally unstable. After all, the first rule of off roading is to be in control. It can be difficult to climb out of well-worn ruts and if they become too deep you could find yourself running out of ground clearance. The result can be that the entire vehicle bellies out (particularly if you are going too fast!) or the front diff. carves out a channel until only jacking up the front will relieve it.

Ridges should be approached at an angle (see Fig. 4.12), making sure you know your ground clearance and the position of the diffs.. Look out for large rocks and if you think you can, drive over them remembering the rear diff.'s position and keeping the vehicle straight as you go over (see Fig. 4.14). If you cannot pass over the rocks without your underneath touching them, it might be preferable to drive the wheels over them.

Travelling at speed off road may be exhilarating but it will be damaging to both vehicle and passengers. Roofs and sides may be padded but a severe blow to the head can occur if a rock or hole is hit suddenly at speed. Picking your way slowly will also allow your exhaust to survive longer.

Fig. 4.10 With top heavy loads and uneven surfaces, even shallow angles need extra care. Passengers are out steadying the sides
Fig. 4.11 A 12-ply steel-braced radial that has blown-out after extensive off-road use. Check your tyres regularly

On some rocky tracks corrugations produce an unpleasant ride. It can be like driving over corrugated iron, so regular are the ridges. Such corrugations are typical of long-distance routes where there is a steady flow of heavy traffic, for example in parts of Scandinavia and also in desert regions. The problem *can* be alleviated by driving at speed, because then the tyres skim over the tops of the ridges and bumps are subsequently reduced. The dilemma that now faces you is the lack of stability and the impossibility of cornering. With virtually no contact with the ground, it is like being on ice: braking distances are considerably increased and sudden cornering will cause rolling.

Summary

- engage FWD on very rough ground and hills
- watch ground clearance, especially beneath diffs.
- drive wheels over rocks if necessary
- keep your speed down

Fig. 4.12 Crossing this ridge at an angle decreases the ramp breakover angle. Coupled with excellent axle articulation, it enables this Land Rover 110 to keeping going

Fig. 4.13 Straddling ruts. Try to keep the vehicle as level as possible, then all wheels have an equal chance of gripping

Fig. 4.14 Knowing the position of your vehicle's diff. can help you negotiate quite large obstacles. If you are unsure of the clearance, it is sometimes better to drive wheels directly over the obstacle

Fig. 4.15 How not to cross a ditch. Taking it head on results in both bumper and chassis grounding
Fig. 4.16 How to cross a ditch. At an angle of 45 degrees only one wheel enters the ditch at a time, thereby avoiding grounding

CROSSING DITCHES

Whether it is a ditch or just a deep hole that bars your route the essential precept is to keep three wheels driving. This can be achieved by only dropping one wheel into a ditch at a time. Always approach and cross at an angle of approximately 45 degrees, taking it slowly in a low gear (see Figs. 4.15 and 4.16). Not only does this maintain maximum traction it will also prevent the chassis grounding. Tackling it from a right angle will drop both front wheels into the ditch with the distinct possibility of causing damage to the bodywork behind those wheels. The front bumper will nose-dive into the far side of the ditch and prevent continued forward movement. Poor approach and departure angles will, of course, increase the problems. The better the axle articulation the deeper the ditch that can ordinarily be negotiated.

Summary

- slow down
- select low gear
- cross at a 45 degree angle
- one wheel in the ditch at a time

DRIVING GULLIES

An 'interesting' obstacle, usually encountered in upland areas, is the V-shaped gully. This is where the track has been washed out by high rainfall, and continuous erosion results in a gully shaped in a V-section. Narrow, rainwashed gullies are a common phenomenon and can be negotiated by having the wheels on either side of the drop (but beware of such conditions on sandstone as the sides can cave in).

But gullies widen and deepen as they progress and can then be dangerous. They must be tackled with caution, and as for any off-road situation, you should walk it first. To drive up or down a gully you should select low range (the choice of gear will depend on whether you are climbing, descending or driving level) and proceed very slowly, keeping one wheel on each side of the gully at a similar level. Ensure that the steering remains straight and that you do not start to climb the gully wall with one wheel. The moment this occurs

Fig. 4.17   When negotiating a deep gully use a passenger to guide the driver

stop and reverse just enough to realign the front wheels. Continuing to climb the side of the gully will result in trapping the vehicle on its side. It can happen very quickly and the extensive body damage that occurs will be just one of your problems – it will be a long and difficult recovery.

If you have a passenger it would be most sensible if they climbed out of the vehicle and helped! A person directing from outside, standing in front, will have a metre or more vision in front of the vehicle than the driver. They should walk a little way ahead to guide you as they can see precisely where your wheels are located and whether a stone or boulder will cause the steering to change lock. Do agree a hand-signal code before you begin. A simple system is for the person walking backwards to raise both arms and beckon with both hands if the vehicle is to proceed straight on. Beckoning with the left hand only signifies steering to the right and beckoning with the right hand, to the left. Needless to say, the driver must trust the person's directions, concentrating on him or her and not on the gully.

Fig. 4.18 Negotiating a gully. Note the nearside wheels pushed wheels hard against gully wall. If these wheels slip down the result would be side body damage

Summary

- walk it first
- select low range
- let passenger direct
- proceed very slowly, following passenger directions only
- keep steering straight

SOFT GROUND

This term includes sand, shingle, mud and snow. The first of these is quite different from the rest and it is often the most difficult to cross, particularly when in the form of dry sand dunes. Sand requires flotation rather than grip on the surface. (For example, Michelin XCL tyres are quite exceptional in mud but almost useless in sand.) Normally one would not encounter this type of ground in any quantity; were you to do so, then sand tyres might be a safe option. (See page 64.)

Fig. 4.19 A Range Rover negotiating very soft mud. Note the slow and steady progress. The pre-attached rope is a sensible precaution

Lowering the tyre pressures is one way of dealing with soft ground. They can be reduced to about half of the normal working pressure and the increased flotation, because of the greater surface area that deflation produces, may be sufficient to keep you moving. Remember to inflate your tyres back to the original pressure as soon as you have left the soft ground. Sand ladders are expensive but represent another effective way of crossing very soft ground. If you are going to use them first of all dig a ramp out of the sand or mud for all wheels, making sure that none of the underbelly of the vehicle is touching the ground. Then place the ladders in front of the rear wheels. The ramp will then assist the wheels in gaining traction on to the ladder. Once mobile the driver must keep going until firmer ground is reached. Always mark the position of sand ladders with the shovel so that you can go back on foot and find the ladders which are very likely to have been buried.

Sand ladders are made from galvanised steel or aluminium. Perforated steelplate (PSP) has been used extensively in the Sahara since the Second World War and a pair of ladders made from this will be essential for any dune crossings. It can be purchased as a 4-m length and then cut in two. Sand mats are a poorer option but can be effective.

Gears

Firstly, the gear that you take on any soft ground is very important because once selected it is usually the one with which you are lumbered. Changing gear either up or down in low range is virtually impossible when crossing soft ground. When you pass through neutral the considerable drag that the terrain has on the wheels will virtually cause the vehicle to stop. As the engine picks up the gear you have selected the wheels will react by spinning. Therefore forward momentum must be maintained.

So, the rule is: select the highest gear that can pull your vehicle through to the other side. This will depend on the power of your engine and the overall gearing of the transfer box. The typical gear to use would be second, low range. This is a good starting point until you are fully aware of your vehicle's potential. A Range Rover would normally cope in third gear but only practice will tell. First gear will nearly always be too low – the wheel rotates so fast that traction is lost and wheel spin is induced. Experience will help you read the track ahead.

On the move

Work on the principle that a level vehicle has better traction. If one side drops then it becomes heavier as the weight shifts to those wheels. Friction is greater and the vehicle pulls to that side. The wheels on the high side become lighter and are more likely to spin. By walking and checking any slope beforehand you should be able to pick a suitable route.

Choosing a route through mud
Study Fig. 4.20. The object is to cross the mud to the far side where there is a sharp left turn up a slippery bank, behind the trees in the centre background. Three possible routes could be taken.

Route 1 This route looks less muddy than the others. However, there is a sharp turn needed at the far end and to slow down for this would cause you to lose the momentum necessary to climb the slippery bank.

Route 2 Through the centre seems the best option. A blast straight through the mud would not result in having to slow down to take the left-hand turn, and momentum can thus be maintained to climb the slippery bank.

Fig. 4.20 Which way to go? Three possible routes, but 2 is best (see text)

Route 3   Less mud is present here but the terrain is more rutted and uneven. The vehicle would have to pass through with two wheels high up on the dry parts, thus resulting in heavy and light wheels. The light wheels are then more likely to spin and lose traction.

Keeping on the move in mud
As well as the sensation of pumping adrenalin it is a sinking in the stomach that one feels when, in the very middle of what appears to be a sea of mud, the revs begin to die and forward motion begins to wane. You must now do everything in your power to keep going because once you have stopped and lost momentum you could be in for a very messy recovery (you are probably already putting your welly boots on!) Fortunately, there are some tricks that can keep you going.

First of all, move the steering wheel from side to side as quickly as possible and maintain this until you are out the other side. This simple technique need only involve a quarter of a turn on the steering wheel, but it presses the wall of the tyre harder into the soft ground and gives more traction. A second trick is to blip the throttle on and off. Don't keep your boot down hard as the wheels will probably spin faster than the vehicle can travel forward and the tyre tread will clog up with the mud. Even if the tread pattern encourages self-cleaning it can be assisted by a sudden change in speed, hence the blipping action. This could be sufficient to throw the clogging material out of the tread.

These two tricks carried out together as you cross soft ground are quite effective. If you do cease forward motion then climb out and have a look rather than throttling away. Half a second extra on the 'loud' pedal when you are not moving will dig the vehicle down into the ground very quickly (in which case, see Chapter 5).

Sand, shingle and snow
Although the basics are very similar to mud, select as high a gear as possible and use very low throttle. Sand that has been wet and is setting usually has a slightly harder crust on the top. Careful driving with no wheel spin should be enough to get you through without breaking through the surface. If the sand is very soft and dry (top surface is light in colour) then you might find a fast dash will give you the momentum to traverse it.

It may be necessary to charge a snowdrift to get through. If this is unsuccessful you will find yourself perched high and dry on top and digging will be required to extricate yourself. Check the depth of snow first if possible. If venturing out into very cold snowy conditions, make sure that you are prepared with survival materials (e.g. emergency food, blankets), as well as self-recovery equipment. If you become stranded in a blizzard and you are not sure that shelter is near at hand, stay with your vehicle. Keep the engine running and the heater on but ensure adequate ventilation. This will probably necessitate the clearing of snow around the exhaust tail-pipe to prevent carbon monoxide poisoning. If the snow becomes very deep think of putting a marker above the vehicle which will give away its location.

When driving on snow, remember that braking distances are multiplied considerably.

Reversing out

If, after all your efforts to keep going, the wheels begin to spin and you stop moving, do not bog yourself in by continued hard throttling. Climb out and have a look. Rather than plough in to the soft ground any more it may be possible to reverse out. Reverse gears on most vehicles tend to be of a lower ratio than second and this may cause the dreaded wheel spin, digging you in deeper. So try a transfer to high ratio reverse gear. This will produce less spin but remember to have FWD and, if fitted, centre diff. lock engaged.

Overdrive is a useful accessory on these occasions. Selecting this with any of the gears will produce a higher ratio and thereby reduce wheel spin. The times when driving out is impossible are those when you are glad of the company of a second vehicle. It is important to have thought, in advance, of having good tow points fitted to the vehicle – make sure this includes the front as well as the rear. Ideally, a strong tow hitch should be attached to both sides of the front chassis. The bolts on these tow points must be checked occasionally to ensure that they are firm.

Summary

- get out and look
- try to gauge depth and slope
- select highest gear, low range, that will pull vehicle through
- try side-to-side steering and blipping of throttle if wheels slip

- if forward motion ceases, throttle off, get out and look. Try reverse gear low range, overdrive engaged if fitted, then high range with FWD, diff. lock if fitted

Note: If you find yourself regularly having to cross very soft, boggy ground a number of people recommend Bog-Cogs. These attachments, which fit to the side of the four wheel, increases yet further the width of surface area trying to spread the load across the substrate. They take up a fair amount of space in the back of the motor when not in use but may be considered a useful addition to the equipment checklist.

WATER

The depth to which you can safely wade will vary from vehicle to vehicle. To obtain some idea of this consult your vehicle handbook. Although you should try not to exceed the stipulated depth for your vehicle, most in actual fact will go through deeper water if really necessary. Ensure that basic waterproofing and wading plugs have been checked. (See page 73.)

Checking the water

There is nothing quite as embarrassing as racing your vehicle into water, with numerous onlookers enjoying the show, only to reach halfway and have the engine die.

Before crossing water there are several aspects to look for. Always try to gauge the depth. If you are likely to be confronted by a regular barrage of water crossings then carry a pole, such as a broom handle, marked at intervals. This can be used to probe the bottom of a river or pool. If help is not likely to be at hand then wading on foot should be tried, probing in front of you with your stick or pole. Find a route that avoids boulders and occasional deeper patches, and look for any submerged hazards such as barbed wire. If wading on foot is out of the question and the water is too deep or too wide to prevent probing, look for any vegetation, gates or telegraph poles nearby that may give an indication of depth.

Very fast flowing sections of a river can cause loss of traction. Where the river narrows it will have a stronger current and so it could be advisable to go for a wider crossing where the current is weaker and the depth at a minimum. However, a compromise has to be reached: flowing water can be easier to cross than still water. The

Fig. 4.21 If practical wade with a stick to check the water depth

latter encourages silt deposition. It may look shallow but what appears to be half a metre deep might have the same depth again in sticky silt – almost guaranteeing bogging down. If the water is moving but with an unbroken surface it will be deep. On the other hand, rippling water on the move will be near to a stony bottom with enough current to sweep away silt. This is the ideal crossing site. Braided rivers, typical of glaciated regions, have small islands of alluvial material. Thus a crossing can be broken up into a series of stages, each one being checked as you go. Make sure you do not become bogged down in the soft alluvium.

After studying the water, check the approach and departure points. Look to see if the track changes direction under the water and where it emerges on the banks. Young rivers in upland regions have a habit of changing direction. If there is no distinct bank then do not necessarily follow the tracks of previous vehicles. Look for an approach that takes a gradual angle. One that is too steep will dip the engine fan into the water. This will spray water around the engine compartment and swamp it before the vehicle has become level in the river (see Fig. 4.22).

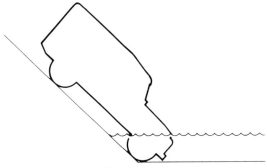

Fig. 4.22 This approach is too steep for entering water. It will result in a swamped engine

Wading through

Before entering the water make sure you are clear where to emerge on the other side. This is not the sort of decision to make in the middle of the river. Your best attempt to exit is your first attempt. If you fail first time it will entail reversing back into the water. In addition, the bank will now be wetter than it was before as the vehicle has dripped over it. A gradual approach and departure angle is needed.

First gear, low range is ideal when there is a firm base on which to cross. It will give the necessary power, keep the revs up and the exhaust blowing out the water. Second gear, low range should be used if silt is going to be encountered or the exit bank is steep and slippery. A vehicle holds on to a tremendous volume of water when crossing a river and this will pour from the underside as you climb the bank. So, what may seem a dry ascent on the far side can quickly become very slippery, particularly if another vehicle is to cross.

Drive slowly in the water and without stopping. By judging your speed right you will create a bow wave as the water hits the front bumper and radiator. (If it splashes over the top of the bonnet on to the windscreen you are driving too fast, and shortly afterwards the engine will probably only fire on two or three cylinders!) Once the bow wave has formed it should be maintained with a steady speed, pushing the water away (see Fig. 4.23). The wall of water in front then creates a low eddy in the engine compartment. This eddy continues along the side to include the front door panels and can assist in stopping water entry under the doors. By stopping in mid-channel the water will soon return to its higher level. Most door seals will allow some water to enter and it is advisable to keep personal effects off the floor! If you do ship water then open the doors on the other side to vent the vehicle. So important is the bow

101

Fig. 4.23   Maintaining the correct bow wave

wave that you must maintain it – if you do lose one cylinder as you cross be prepared to slip the clutch. Keep the revs up and the vehicle going at all costs.

When crossing fast-flowing water it is better to head slightly down-stream; you will not present such a flat side to the current and will therefore take less water into the engine compartment.

Needless to say, if there is a group of vehicles they should cross one at a time.

Diesel engines
Vehicles powered by diesel engines are better than petrol ones for wading in deep water. This is due to their sealed fuel system and lack of electrics to make them fire. However, both petrol and diesel engines will suffer if water gets to the cylinders. This is especially catastrophic with the high compression diesel engine where water does not compress. This can damage either conrods or crankshaft.

Water entry to the cylinders stops the engine dead. Do not try to start it with either the starter motor or towing. Instead, remove the plugs or injectors. Then turn the engine over with the starter motor or, if available, a starting handle. This should pump any water out of the cylinders.

102

Fig. 4.24 The air intake of a Camel Trophy Land Rover, raised for deep water wading

Air intakes and fans

The position of the air intake in relation to the engine is a limiting factor in wading, so be aware of its location. Expensive extension pipes can be purchased (like those used in the Camel Trophy), but a cheap alternative can be constructed from household plastic piping and brackets. Hose-like extensions can be fitted to the exhaust pipe which clip on to the roof guttering. Generally, this is unnecessary as long as your vehicle does not stall in very deep water.

As already mentioned, engine fans can cause a problem by spraying the engine compartment with water if the angle of entry to the river is too steep. If there is no alternative or the water is so deep that spray from the fan is inevitable, then slacken off the alternator attachment bolts prior to crossing. This will permit the fan belt to slip on the fan pulley so that less water will be flicked back towards the electrics. Remember to tighten the bolts soon after the crossing as cooling as well as electricity generation will be affected.

Brakes

Most people forget that brakes are less effective after driving through water. You must establish the habit of checking them soon after crossing. Drum brakes are worse than disc brakes. If the efficiency has been impaired then drive for a while with your foot on the brake until the drum has warmed up sufficiently to encourage drying.

Occasionally when a vehicle stops in the middle of a water crossing you may need to use the handbrake. Unless this works off the prop shaft there is no certainty of it holding.

Summary

- gauge depth and decide suitable route
- check opposite bank for a good exit
- fit wading plug (if any) and check all other waterproofing measures
- select first gear, low range (second if surface soft)
- drive slowly into water, do not stop; maintain a steady, slow speed to obtain a bow wave
- when across, remove wading plug (if any)
- check brakes

5

Self-Recovery
Techniques

Even with experience and the best technique, everyone eventually gets into a situation which prevents them simply driving out. Mistakes are easily made and off-road conditions change so quickly. Being caught in a sudden deluge of rain could turn your pleasant Sunday afternoon green laning into a battle through a quagmire more reminiscent of the Somme. Even after dry periods, tracks can become hazardous due to the cracking earth. This makes the ground unstable and the weight of a vehicle on the edge of deep ruts could be enough to cause them to give way. If several vehicles are in convoy the last one invariably suffers from the crumbling surfaces weakened by the leaders. It is therefore paramount that all off roaders prepare themselves for the eventuality of becoming stuck. Two or more vehicles together will lessen the problem but even then some basic equipment is required.

The bare essentials are: a shovel, a rope of the right type and a high-lift jack. These are the off roader's insurance. Most situations can be dealt with using the three singly or combined. Compared to a winch they are considerably cheaper and infinitely more versatile, though under certain conditions a winch may recover a bogged vehicle more quickly than would these bare essentials. Handled correctly, the winch will take a vehicle across obstacles that driving could never do. Both self-recovery techniques have their place in off roading but a winch must be considered a non-essential item unless you anticipate following in the wake of the Camel Trophy! Let us look at these essentials one by one.

Fig. 5.1 Basic recovery equipment

THE SHOVEL

A spade is a spade! Or is it? Military surplus stores sell ex-army shovels, which have the best shape – tapering to a point. Most shovels have wooden handles and shafts, but these become brittle as they dry out and have an annoying tendency to snap at the worst possible time. In addition, an off roader's shovel is likely to be abused (used as a lever, etc.), so a steel shaft is preferable. All-steel spades can be purchased from DIY stores and then, if necessary, the base can be tapered with an angle grinder.

Different conditions warrant different types of shovel. For example, ones with short handles are very good in sand as normally you will find yourself digging on your knees. A longer handle does help, however, when trying to remove sand from under a long wheelbase vehicle. In Scandinavian countries they use long-handled shovels as depth measurers for rivers and more specifically in Iceland they employ a long pole handle, painted with stripes at 5 cm intervals.

THE ROPE

A good strong rope is one of the essential pieces of kit for the off roader. It is a fairly common sight to see some of these people with a hemp rope draped around their front bumper or bull bar. This has a degree of pose value but has a number of drawbacks. It is certainly important to stow the rope in a place from where it can be easily collected but this should also be clean. Hemp rots quickly if it gets wet and muddy. In fact, man-made fibre is preferable to hemp as it will not rot. Mud and sand in any rope will, if it is used regularly, cause it to deteriorate as the grit abrades the fibre. Keep it clean.

The KERR technique

The rope needs to have a breaking strain of about 10 tons. Polypropylene is strong and does not stretch. This is known as a 'dead' rope and is suitable for straightforward towing. It is also ideal for attachment to a hand winch (or high-lift jack). Nylon rope is different in that it can stretch and is therefore unsuitable for winching.

Fig. 5.2 Abandon ship! A vehicle stuck in quicksand, like this, can be speedily recovered by using the KERR method

However, this stretching property can be used in a potentially very dangerous but efficacious recovery technique. This uses a snatch rope or Kinetic Energy Recovery Rope (KERR for short). The rope must be of the correct type: nylon with a breaking strain of 22,000 lb or 12 tons. It may or may not be plaited but the former is preferable as it is easier to inspect for damage. This type of rope can stretch to 40 per cent more than its original length (before it breaks) and when stretched has stored within it a considerable amount of energy – enough to suck out a severely bogged vehicle that no other method can extract.

Several snatch ropes are available on the market and one of the latest is a hi-tech rope produced by H & T Marlow Ltd, called Recoverline (see Useful Addresses). This has an 8-strand, multi-plait construction and can be used with connecting ropes (called a bridle) to attach the snatch rope to the vehicle. The bridle rope is threaded through the loop of the snatch rope and then the ends of the bridle are connected to strong attachment points either side of the vehicle. This has the effect of halving the strain of the pull on each side.

The KERR technique requires the attachment of the snatch rope to the stuck vehicle. This point of attachment must be firm – preferably a suitable tow hitch connected to the chassis. If not, it can be connected to the spring hangers on vehicles with leaf suspension. The recovery vehicle is then backed up as close as possible without the risk of becoming stuck itself. The other end of the rope is attached to the back of this vehicle and the remaining slack laid on the ground in a snake formation so that it will readily pay out behind the recovery vehicle without snagg-

Fig. 5.3   A chain sling used as a bridle

ing or knotting. The recovery vehicle now drives off in low range gears, accelerating up to its maximum permitted speed. (The manufacturer recommends that a vehicle up to 2 tons in weight should not exceed 12 mph.) The rope goes tight but it has the effect of using the weight of both vehicles multiplied by the speed. When fully stretched there is a considerable potential energy in the rope, and like a length of elastic it pulls back and de-bogs the stranded vehicle.

Without seeing (and feeling) the pull this might seem a very violent recovery method, but because of the considerable stretch in the rope it is surprisingly smooth. There are a tremendous number of forces operating in this recovery. It is essential that all attachments and bolts on vehicles employed are strong and in excellent condition, e.g. no rusted chassis in the area of connection. Even if you are convinced of this fact keep all passengers and bystanders well clear.

Fig. 5.4   The KERR method being effectively used

It is not unknown for attachment points to shear off and catapult the tow hitch along the axis of the rope. The forces are quite exceptional. So be warned, because they can kill or maim.

If the stuck vehicle is heavily bogged then the recovery can be improved by putting it in first gear low range so that the wheels are slowly rotating. Do this only if necessary because there is a danger that if the vehicle suddenly gets traction and drives over the rope it could wind around the front axle. At the very least this will tear out the brake pipes and at worst pull off the axle. When extracting a well-bogged vehicle it may be necessary for the recovery vehicle to perform a series of snatches.

The KERR method can still be used when there is no other vehicle as long as you have a hand winch or a high-lift jack. Put the stuck vehicle in gear with the handbrake on. Connect the snatch rope to the vehicle and the winch or high-lift jack. The latter must then be firmly attached to an anchor point such as a tree or rock so that there is a minimum of slack. Using the winch or jack, stretch the rope as much as possible. This will effectively store energy in the rope. Drive the vehicle forward, releasing the handbrake at the same time.

With the assistance of the rope pulling back on itself there should be enough power to move the vehicle half a metre to a metre while you steer straight. Repeating this two or three times will probably be sufficient to get you out of trouble.

It should be stressed again that although the KERR technique is a very efficient recovery method it can be very dangerous. Make sure all persons nearby are aware of the moment when the recovery is about to take place.

THE HIGH-LIFT JACK

Designed for lifting heavy machinery and loads it was almost inevitable that the high-lift jack would become an essential tool for the off roader. It is probably the single most useful piece of equipment you can carry on your vehicle but, like any mechanical device, it must be treated with a certain amount of respect. The main use to which it can be put is for direct self-recovery; indirectly, it can be modified to operate as a winch and a more mundane use is for lifting the vehicle when changing a wheel. Other, rather specific, uses include breaking tyre seals when in remote regions, as a clamp, and for spreading or closing bodywork. The jack should come with an attachment that bolts on to the end of the column at a right angle. This can then be used as a clamp.

The high-lift jack is truly a very versatile piece of equipment. Check the suitability of your nudge/bull bar and bumper's ability to be jacked up by the high-lift jack. The tow hitch at the rear can also be used.

The principle behind the high-lift mechanism is that the moving jack climbs the column, moving up one hole at a time with each downward action of the handle. As the jack climbs so two pins alternately pull in and out of the holes in the column. A lever on one side of the jack changes the direction of travel to descend the column. This should be released when the handle is in the upward and closed position.

Typically, high-lift jacks come in two sizes: 4 ft and 5 ft. The difference in cost between the 4- or 5-foot models is minimal, but the shorter is quite adequate for most needs. The extra length can be useful when hand winching although, in the purchase of the jack, storage could be the deciding factor.

Fig. 5.5 A classic recovery situation. Using the high-lift jack to suspend the vehicle, material can be packed under the rutted wheel

When buying a new or secondhand jack check for good quality and that it is not a cheap copy. First of all look at the foot and body of the jack, the section that does the lifting and holds the working parts. These parts must be made from cast steel not pressed steel. A number of versions are available in pressed steel but cannot stand up to sustained, rough handling. Having said that, the base should be of pressed steel as this will be more resilient if the jack tilts to one side during its operation.

If you start with a new jack, some work must be done on it to improve its efficiency. Usually, burrs are present around the holes and they may restrict the free movement of the pins as the jack moves. Clean any paint off the column and rub a flat file down both sides where the holes have been punched. Oil the column and all moving parts regularly. Get to know the jack well. Familiarise yourself with its operation by trying it out on different parts of the bumper.

Using the high-lift jack

It will come as no surprise that this jack is an unstable structure when in use. The higher you lift the vehicle the more unstable it becomes. Consequently never lie underneath a vehicle when it has been lifted unless axle stands or other safe props have been installed. The jack is stable enough to change a wheel although it is essential to engage low range FWD, in gear with handbrake and diff. locks (if fitted) on. Changing a wheel is easy when using a high-lift jack as, unlike a bottle- or screw-jack, no clambering under the vehicle is necessary. In addition, there is no concern over the depth of space for inserting the jack under the axle. An adaptor is made for more recent Land Rovers, which bolts on to the lifting foot and mates with the jacking holes in the chassis.

When the vehicle is bogged down and the mud is flying the high-lift comes into its own. Two methods can be employed. In both cases place the jack in the centre of the rear bumper or cross-member and lift both wheels clear of the ground; if it is rutted then continue until they are above the top of the rut. This should be possible with the height and lifting capacity of the jack.

The first method of recovery is to fill ground ruts with rocks, wood or anything that will give grip. After lowering the vehicle back on to the ground it should be possible to drive out. If it is still severely stuck it may be necessary to repeat the exercise at the front of the vehicle. This technique can also be used when the chassis or suspension bellies out on a deeply-rutted track. Once you have packed the ruts with material use the shovel to clear a way through for the front wheels to climb out of the rut on to better terrain.

The second recovery method turns the unstable characteristic of the high-lift jack into a positive advantage. When the wheels are as high as possible above the ground, instead of placing material under the wheels (invariably nothing can be found just when you need it) the jack is collapsed sideways by simply pushing the side of the vehicle. The degree of bogging will determine how many times the operation will have to be repeated. By alternating front and rear the vehicle can be moved, crab fashion, to the side of the ruts on to firmer ground.

One possible problem with using the jack in soft terrain is that it will just sink as you try to lift the vehicle. All that is needed is something that can increase the surface area of the base. A base extension that can be made very simply is a piece of strong wood approximately half a metre square and several centimetres thick. To

Fig. 5.6 Recovery by collapsing the jack. First, the supported vehicle is lifted as high as possible, then, with helpers well clear, it is moved sideways on to firm ground

hold the base of the jack in position four strips of wood can be fixed to form a rectangle in the centre of the square. Alternatively, use your shovel: it can be just as successful although it does limit your options if it is needed after the jacking procedure. A spare wheel also makes an ideal base.

Safety

There is a lever on the moving foot of the jack which reverses the body lifting mechanism. It points up for lifting and down for lowering. Never leave the lever in the down position with a load suspended on the jack. Only have it in that position when operating the handle for lowering. If the vehicle is knocked the jack could slip or work itself down the column, which is not only inconvenient but can be extremely dangerous as the handle will be thrown up and down by the weight of the load. A number of accidents, including broken jaws, have been caused by flying handles. For the same reason, do not be tempted to change the position of the lever unless you first have your right hand on the operating handle, which should be in the upright position. If the jack is to hold a load for any amount of time you can always fit a shackle through the first visible hole in the column below the lifting foot.

Hand winching with the high-lift jack

Using the jack as a winch is not hard work and has extricated many stricken off roaders. The length of pull is limited by the length of travel on the jack. On the plus side it is very powerful and the rope can be shortened at intervals so that another bite at the recovery can be made. Two ropes or chains are required, or you may get away with only one if a direct connection can be made to the vehicle. Attach one end of a rope or chain to the top of the column by a shackle. Connect the other end to an anchor point, e.g. a tree. The second rope or chain is attached by a shackle to the climbing foot of the jack which should be located at the bottom of the column. The other end of this rope or chain is then attached to the tow point of the vehicle. Make sure the ropes or chains are as taut as possible with the jack held up in the middle. Then slowly move the jack up the column. If a second attempt is required, secure the vehicle so that it will not return to its original position while you slide the jack to the bottom of the column and shorten the rope.

It is of course possible that no tree or fixed object is nearby. This is where ground anchors (see page 120) are important. In an

Fig. 5.7   Using the high lift jack as a winch

emergency it may be possible to use the spare wheel, buried at 45 degrees, as a ground anchor.

Many people mount their high-lift jack on the outside of the vehicle because of the length. The 5-ft jack will fit across the back of a Land Rover roof. Covers can be obtained but the jacks will survive mud, wind and rain, so long as you remember to oil and clean the mechanism occasionally.

Air jacks

In principle, air jacks are excellent but in practice they are limited. They are, however, ideal for the smaller 4x4 vehicle, especially where a high-lift jack is not easy to carry.

The air jack is a bag with a tube connected to the exhaust pipe. The bag is placed under the vehicle so that as the engine ticks over the bag inflates, lifting the vehicle. Logs or brushwood could be placed under the wheels or body once the bag has lifted the vehicle clear of the ground. The main disadvantages are that the larger air jacks may bend or collapse into a V, they must be kept clear of hot exhaust pipes underneath the vehicle and mud needs to be cleaned off the bag before stowing. The bag must not kink and it must be folded correctly so that when required for use it will unfold correctly.

WINCHING

Winches are good but not that good! Like any machinery, the winch is only as effective as its operator. It is a specialist piece of equipment which can be a useful insurance when driving off road but such insurance can tempt you to be less cautious and go further than you should. For the experienced winchman this will probably just increase the journey time. For the inexperienced person it can be downright dangerous. There are occasions when a winch can be essential but, for no other reason than the enormous outlay of funds, think carefully before investing in a winch. Then consider a course in winching so that you can receive the very best instruction from an expert.

Winching safety

Winches are potentially dangerous and must be treated with care.

First, buy a set of heavy-duty gloves and keep these stored in your vehicle. The industrial, waterproof type are particularly good because the rope or cable invariably becomes wet and caked in mud. They must be used when paying out the cable on the winch.

Second, try not to stand between the stuck vehicle and the anchor point. If the cable were to snap it could be lethal. For this very reason regularly check the cable for fraying and cuts. Even loose strands can cut the fingers to the bone. Use a cable with a swaged end. This means that the tip of the cable is bent back on itself around a thimble and then joined by a sleeve that is power pressed tightly on to the cable. If alternative cable joiners are used make sure that a thimble is employed and that the gripping part of the clip is on the 'live' side of the cable (i.e. on the length doing the pulling). The U-bolts that go through the cast grips must be on the 'dead' side. Clean the cable with a light oil occasionally.

Third, remember never to step over the cable, rope or chain that spans the gap between the stuck vehicle and anchor point/other vehicle. Even if the line is lying slack on the ground there is always a chance that it may suddenly be pulled taut just as you step over it, ending with the obvious, painful result. To avoid this, walk around the back of the vehicle or anchor points. Circumstances do occur when this is impossible or impractical. In this situation step on the line so that if it unexpectedly goes tight it will just throw you off.

The winch operator has the responsibility to ensure that the cable is winding on to the winch drum smoothly and straight. He must warn all other personnel that the winching is to take place and keep them clear of the line. A recovery may seem particularly heavy, causing an apparent strain on the line. In this instance, it will be the attachment point (as long as the cable has been checked regularly) that is most likely to break. Carry a blanket in the vehicle (a coat will do) so that when winching this can be draped over the opposite end of the line. If the attachment or cable were to break the blanket would act like a drag chute and stop the cable before it reached you.

When a cable breaks free under strain it recoils in a large spiral and can kill or maim. With regular inspection and by not overloading the manufacturer's stated maximum weight limit it will be quite safe. It is the unknown factor, the attachment point on the other vehicle, which is the cause for concern. Check that the area is not rusted and that any bolts are in good condition.

Summary of safety

- wear heavy-duty gloves
- inspect the winch cable regularly for fraying and cuts
- do not stand near cable or step across it
- in emergency only, cross line by stepping on it
- check attachment point is strong
- cover end of cable with a blanket in case of whiplash

Winch types

The variety and diversity of winches is seemingly complicated. In fact, the classification of the different types is straightforward. At the start one can identify two forms: the powered winch and the hand winch. The latter will be dealt with at the end of this section on winches. Of the former type, three varieties are available:

Hydraulic winch

These are expensive and complicated. They are not necessary for the general off roader and are not really intended for self-recovery but more for moving heavy loads such as timber. They are very powerful, can be mounted anywhere on the vehicle and will run almost continuously.

Mechanical winch
Mounted in front of the radiator the mechanical winch takes its power from either the transfer box or from the front of the engine. The former connection has the advantage of being more versatile as the gearbox is used to select different speeds and will run continuously.

Electric winch
This is probably the most practical winch for self-recovery off road due to its simplicity. It is powered by a motor about the size of a starter motor which drives through a small gearbox to achieve the desired speed reduction. The control switch is usually a remote one on the end of a wire that plugs on to the winch prior to use. This makes recovery very straightforward. All you have to do is put the winch in neutral, pay out the cable and ensure that it is safely anchored at the opposite end. Then sit in the vehicle to drive and steer whilst operating the winch with the remote control. It is worth anticipating the need for the winch prior to becoming bogged down

Fig. 5.8 Winching up a slope. Note use of snatch block in double rigging to increase the pulling power

as the remote lead needs to be plugged into the machinery. Under water or in mud this can be a difficult operation, so remember to plug in before entering the obstacle.

The electric winch can drain a battery in minutes, so whatever vehicle the winch is mounted on ensure you keep the engine running. If the vehicle is stationary it may be necessary to put a rock on the throttle to maintain the charge. Most electric winches differ in the load they can pull so make sure it is compatible with your vehicle. A little more power is better than being borderline when bogged in very glutinous mud.

A very useful and effective self-recovery winch now on the market is an electric portable. Although it is not particularly powerful it will be quite sufficient for the average recovery situation. Rated at 3,000 lb pulling power it is most effective when double rigged (see Fig. 5.8). It attaches to the vehicle by being mounted on a tow ball, front or rear. This enables it to swing in line with the cable and anchor so that it always winds evenly on to the drum. The electric leads connect on to the vehicle battery and when not in use the entire winch can simply be dismantled and stowed in the boot or rear of your 4x4.

Anchoring points and ground anchors

The winch is only as good as the anchor at the other end of the line. Natural anchors that may be available are trees and rocks. When using a tree the bark must be protected from any damage. To this end a strop (a nylon strap with a loop at each end) must be employed or a protective sleeve put over a chain. When connecting the strop check the stability of the tree. Evergreens tend to be shallow rooted whilst deciduous varieties will be more stable. For example, an oak with a diameter of 30 cm should sustain a load of 10,000 kg.

Attach the strop to the base of the tree. If a post has been used, pass it twice round the base so that it will grip even if the post leans. A strong chain can be used as an anchor attachment; this is especially useful if it has a self-clipping hook to make it easily adjustable. The inside diameter of each link should be capable of holding three of its own size links. Much wider and the strength will be lost.

Invariably, it seems that when the vehicle gets stuck no strong anchorage is available. Under these conditions you need to consider one of the following types of ground anchor:

Fig. 5.9 A strop for protecting trees, wound twice around the base to

T-stakes

These are made from angle iron in lengths of approximately 60 cm and have a cross-piece welded to one end. A stake is hammered through a large metal ring which is laid on the ground. It is not necessary to drive the stake fully home as the attachment and pull is always from the ring at ground level. However, T-stakes must be used in pairs, roped or chained together (see Fig. 5.10). The more stakes used the more load the anchor will hold. If you do not have proper T-stakes, in an emergency you may be able to improvise by using materials found locally. There is a probability that the improvised anchor will not be as strong, so use more stakes roped together to increase the stability.

Auger anchor

In soft ground, such as peat, the auger anchor will hold a load, but it is unsuitable for other terrain. The auger is like a large corkscrew that has a separate bar to wind the auger into the soft ground.

Flat plate anchors

There are a variety of different forms, most consisting of flat steel plates with a number of holes through which stakes can be driven to fix them to the ground (see Fig 5.11).

121

Fig. 5.10   The arrangement for setting up T-stakes. Note the ring at the base of the first stake for attachment of a winching cable

Danforth anchor

These are sold by weight and come in several sizes. The Danforth is basically a boat anchor. When used in recovery it is very effective but needs someone to stand on it until it digs in sufficiently.

If the winch vehicle is not operating self-recovery then it should be anchored in some way. This could be by attachment either to a tree or ground anchor at the rear or chocks to the front wheels. If these precautions are not taken and only brakes used then the deterioration of the brakes' seals will be rapid.

Power winching

Drum winch

When operating a drum winch it is most important to see that the cable winds on to the drum evenly. The cable passes through a guide called a forelead. This may be just a slit in soft metal, although better ones have rollers on the top and bottom plus other rollers on

Fig. 5.11 Staking a V-shaped ground anchor

Fig. 5.12 Husky electric winch double rigged. Note the chocks (wedgits) under the front wheels to anchor the vehicle

the sides. Bunched cable on one side of the drum must be avoided as this is very damaging and can very quickly destroy the line.

Having purchased a power winch there is an assortment of further accoutrements to acquire. The most important of these is a pulley, or snatch block. This has two uses. A stuck vehicle will rarely be in line with a possible anchor point. (This can be guaranteed!) To begin with, it is possible to use the snatch block to alter the direction of pull. Secondly, the snatch block can be used to increase the pulling power of the winch. The increase is almost 100 per cent. This will then lessen the load on the battery and decrease the speed by about 50 per cent.

The technique is called double rigging and increases the efficiency of all winches. Connect the pulley or snatch block to the anchor point (or vehicle to be recovered if this does not have the working winch). Then pass the winch cable through the block and back to the winching vehicle, or somewhere near the pulling line. For severely bogged vehicles a second block could be employed on the winching

*Fig. 5.13 Realigning the cable on a David Bowyer combination Roo Bar &
Winch mounting kit fitted with a Superwinch X9*
*Fig. 5.14 The rope 'made-off' on a capstan winch. This way the load can
be held safely.*

vehicle and the end of the cable then goes back to attach to the original anchor point.

Capstan winch
Manufactured by Superwinch of Tavistock in Devon, the capstan winch is used mainly on Land Rovers and Range Rovers. It is like a ship's capstan, and sits in front of the radiator, attached to the bumper and chassis. A mechanical winch, it is operated directly from the engine via the front bottom pulley and is engaged by a dog clutch (a lever) located on the winch body. The engine rotates the bollard at a fairly slow pace at tickover speed. A rope is connected to the load and fed under the guide bar on the outside of the winch. The rope is then wound three times around the rotating bollard. Control over the operation is by the degree of tension applied to the unattached end of the rope. Holding this end of the rope, tension is applied on to the bollard and the load is pulled. By easing the rope slack the winching stops and by letting the rope slip backwards the load can be reversed.

Although not as powerful as a drum winch, the capstan winch is infinitely more controllable. It can be worked all day without causing any strain on the equipment or vehicle and as a recovery winch is second to none. However, its disadvantage is that it is not so suitable for self-recovery.

Make sure the rope is the correct type, as supplied by Superwinch, a very special terylene-coated, multi-plait dead rope.

Hand winching
For achieving self-recovery with a step down in price and weight from power winches, but not in efficiency, you should consider the hand winch. (See also page 115 where the high-lift jack is considered as a hand winch.) The advantage of a hand winch is that, although it has to be worked manually, it has the ability to pull at any angle. It is small, light and transportable. Survey the market before you attempt to buy. Some of the hand winches available are just not strong enough to be worth mentioning. Let us look at two types:

Lug-all winch
This is made in the United States and has a cast aluminium body. There are two sizes, the largest of which is quite capable of de-bogging a 2-ton vehicle. A snatch block is fitted as standard to the cable so that the winch can be double rigged. Used in this fashion, with its telescopic extension handle, the Lug-all is very

powerful. It does have some minus points, however, the chief one being the length of its cable. This comes with the winch and, at a little under 6 m for a single pull line and less than 3 m for a double rig pull, it is limited. Letting a load down, too, is slow, but having said that, the machine is nevertheless well engineered, simple to use and easy to clean by hosing down when it gets covered with mud.

Tirfor winch
This winch comes in two parts: the winch body and handle and a separate cable. A lever is pulled back on the body to thread the cable into the winch and only the right cable will fit. One end of this cable has a hook whilst the other end is tapered to allow it to be threaded through the machine. Because the cable can be purchased separately the length can be chosen to fit your requirements. The 30 m length should be adequate for most off-road recovery.

To use the winch the body is attached to an anchor point, for which it has its own hook. The hook on the cable is connected to the vehicle, threading the tapered end into the winch body. The line must come out the other side, clear of the winch, before a locking lever is engaged. Then the handle is worked backwards and

Fig. 5.15 The Tirfor winch in operation

forwards, pulling the line as it goes. Every little effort on the handle achieves results, pulling it through on both strokes whatever the movement. If you wish to reverse the moving cable the handle is removed and attached to the reverse lever. Thus you have a very controllable winch. The lifting lever has shear pins fitted so that if you over-strain the winch you just fail to lift or lower the load but it will remain holding it until you renew the pins.

Bush winching

The chances are that if you are stuck, you are in an emergency situation and will try anything. Any system that can shorten a rope strung between the vehicle and an anchor point could in theory act as a form of hand winch. Just twisting a rope round with a bar can move a stuck vehicle a very short distance. Repeated a number of times, chocking the wheels so that it does not return to the original position, it may be enough to get you out of such an emergency. But it is not ideal, does not always work and can be dangerous.

This bush winch idea has been modified to produce a capstan-type winch which works well. Two strong poles or logs are needed, as well as a length or rope. One of these poles is pushed into the

Fig. 5.16. The 'Bushman's Winch'. The cross pole passes through a loop of the rope and is then turned like a capstan (photo by courtesy of Dave Shephard)

ground midway between the stuck vehicle and an anchor point. One end of the rope is securely fixed to the vehicle. Lay the rope out towards the anchor point. Before attaching the other end wind several turns of the middle of the rope around the pole. As the rope is wound round it, lay the second pole on the rope so that it is attached to the other pole, constructing a cross. While someone holds this in place another person then attaches the other end of the rope to the anchor. Two people then rotate the 'capstan' pole using the cross-piece. As the rope is wound tightly on to the capstan it will, of course, shorten the rope, which then pulls the bogged vehicle clear. This system succeeds with two men in a situation where, ordinarily, they could never hope to pull the vehicle out without further mechanical assistance or manpower.

STRAIN – A USEFUL FORMULA

An estimate of the force required to move a stuck vehicle, by whatever means, can be worked out with a simple formula. Because of the uncertain nature of any recovery technique this can be worth doing, especially if you are trying it for the first time. It will help to confirm that the equipment with which you are working, whether vehicle, anchor points, rope or cable is capable of the strain needed for that recovery. It is useful to think about, even if only to familiarise yourself with the different factors that have to be taken into consideration.

First, work out the ground condition (GC) which is numbered from 2 to 25.

Type of Ground	Ground Condition (GC)
Smooth road	25
Grass	7
Hard wet sand	6
Gravel or soft wet sand	5
Loose dry sand	4
Shingle	3
Soft clay or mud	2

Now take the approximate weight of the vehicle, say 2 tons, and divide by the estimated GC figure. This yields what is called the

Rolling Resistance (RR). For example, if the ground is soft mud it will be 2 divided by 2, giving an RR of 1 ton. This resistance will be affected by the angle at which the stuck vehicle will have to be pulled. A gradient resistance (GR) must be calculated and added to the RR. Even a vehicle on the flat will have a GR because it will have sunk into the mud, probably up to the axles. From the bottom of the wheels to the top of the mud will be at least 30 degrees. For a gradient up to 45 degrees the GR is calculated at a sixtieth of the vehicle weight. Over that angle and the GR is taken as equal to the weight of the vehicle.

For example, if a 2-ton vehicle is stuck in soft mud up to the axles (i.e. the slope is 30 degrees), the force required to extricate it can be calculated as follows:

$$\text{Rolling Resistance} = \frac{\text{vehicle weight}}{\text{ground condition}} \quad \text{i.e.} \quad \frac{2 \text{ tons}}{2} = 1 \text{ ton}$$

Gradient Resistance = weight of vehicle x slope, i.e. 2 x 30 = 60

As this is below 45 degrees it is calculated at a sixtieth (i.e. divide by 60).
Thus the GR is 1, and the force required is RR plus GR, i.e. a total of 2 tons.

A safety factor should be added at the end. This consists of a quarter of the total (RR plus GR). Thus the final total is 2.5 tons. It is practical to round up to the nearest figure so that in this instance a force of 3 tons will be needed to extricate the stuck vehicle. More importantly, the rope or cable and attachment points must be able to cope with this force.

6

Mechanical Failure

Off roading puts stress on the 4x4 and will eventually cause something to break. It will be just your luck that this happens in the middle of nowhere with little or no help around. If you have followed our advice, a second vehicle will be with you so that in an emergency a tow back to civilisation is possible. For this reason you may consider making a solid tow bar or better still a towing 'A' frame. Construct this out of heavy-duty angle iron in the shape of an 'A' with a 50 mm tow hitch coupling at the top. At the bottom of the two legs drill holes for bolts to attach the frame to a pair of towing eyes fitted to the front of the chassis. This is very useful insurance for expeditions that involve several vehicles on prolonged off-road travel. One vehicle carries the frame on its front and all the other vehicles must be fitted with similar fixing eyes so that it can be transferred across as necessary (see Fig. 7.4). The vehicles must also have a 50 mm tow ball at the rear.

These solid tow bars will be able to tow a vehicle hundreds of miles off or on road without the need for brakes. When not in use they can be stood upright against the bonnet, held in place by a rubber bungie or luggage strap.

TIPS TO GET YOU HOME

Broken half-shaft or differential
A noise emanating from the rear axle and a loss of drive suggests a broken half-shaft or differential. Alternatively, it could be worn splines where the half-shaft connects with the drive flange on the wheel. Either way, that axle must be isolated. The drive to the dud axle can be disconnected by removing the rear prop shaft. Then, by engaging FWD (not forgetting any freewheeling hubs), come home with the front wheels driving. As the vehicle is not specifically

designed for front-wheel drive, take it easy. (Note, though, that we have driven fully laden from central Spain to England this way. Wheel spin at traffic lights can draw attention from the locals!)

Vehicles with permanent FWD need to engage the central diff. lock after removing the prop shaft.

Clutch

If the clutch has failed completely there is little one can do but tow the vehicle away. However, a failed clutch-operating mechanism, either mechanical or hydraulic, may be temporarily repaired. Symptoms may suggest a failed clutch but check one or two things first. Earlier models of the Land Rover, for example, have a pinned link from the pedal to the clutch. This could be faulty, and if so can be temporarily repaired with a bolt, nail or piece of wire. An undetected fluid leak from the hydraulics may lead to a loss of pressure resulting in a failed clutch. In an emergency water or even fruit juice could be used.

After checking for the simple things that could be wrong it may still be possible to drive even if the clutch will not disengage. That is to say, it has failed with the transmission engaged so that movement can still occur but not gear changes. Gear changes are possible without the clutch but this action requires skill, especially for reverse. Low range gears can be accessed by selecting a gear with the engine switched off. As you turn the engine over it will start and get you moving.

Gearbox

First and second gears may break in the gearbox, creating a problem when trying to pull away. Try starting off in third gear, low range, and, once running, change up into high range.

Radiator leak

A temporary repair for a leaking radiator is to use the white of an egg (well, there might be a farm nearby!) Add this to the radiator water whilst the engine is running. Other additives that are known to work include porridge and oatmeal.

Petrol tank and fuel system

Whilst crossing rocky ground it is relatively easy to catch the fuel tank on a boulder or sharp rock. The most easily damaged area is around the drain plug or along the seams. Effective temporary plugs

Fig. 6.1 Having broken down off road the Lada is being held by the Land Rover over a gully so that it can be worked on safely

include chewing gum and soap. Both become hard in contact with petrol. Chew the gum until it becomes pliable and push into the holes or cracks. Soap can be rubbed up and down the area to build up several layers. Be prepared to repeat the treatment at intervals.

If the split is severe no gum or soap is going to work. Instead, a temporary and separate fuel tank needs to be improvised. For this you need a petrol can or even an old oil can to act as the fuel reservoir. Into the spout clip the end of the fuel pipe that goes to the carburettor. This should be arranged so that the temporary tank is held at a height above the carburettor, ideally attached to the roof rack so that gravity feeds the fuel. Watch out for airlocks. This system will not only bypass fuel tank and fuel lines but also a fuel pump.

Brakes

Brakes may start to fail because of a leaking wheel cylinder or damage to a brake pipe. This could cause a severe loss of brake fluid which will result in no brakes at all. If you suspect a rapid loss of fluid, track down the leaking area and flatten that brake pipe out.

Then bend it over so that no more fluid loss will occur. This must only be used in an emergency as braking will cause an uneven pull and your stopping power will be seriously impaired.

Fan belt

If charging stops because of a broken or split fan belt and no spare is available, then tights, stockings or any similar material could be utilised. The makeshift belt need not be tied around the alternator (although this can give better tension) but just between the fan and pulley wheel to ensure the vehicle does not overheat. String or twine wound tightly around the two will also work, but make sure there are no loose ends to get caught up.

Windscreen wiper motor

The annoying effects of wiper motor failure can be lessened by attaching two lengths of string to the wiper. One length goes around to the passenger's window and the second in through the driver's. A passenger can then operate the wiper manually from inside the vehicle by pulling the string ends first one way and then the other. (Well, it's novel!)

Chassis breakage

Wood, rope and straps can be bound on to a broken chassis as supports or splints, but this temporary sort of repair is only as good as the tightness of the bindings. Use a system of tourniquets to get them as tight as possible.

7

Towing

A 4x4 vehicle is the usual choice when the ability to tow a large load is required. Conversely, many owners of 4x4s buy with no thought of towing but then want to extend the versatility of their vehicle by using a trailer. Never be tempted to over-stretch your vehicle. The maximum towing weight will be in your vehicle's handbook. However, one should aim to tow less than three-quarters of that weight as prolonged towing will stress the vehicle and cause excessive wear on the transmission and engine. There are strict laws governing the lights and brakes of different types of trailer. It is easy to forget maintenance of the trailer but, like the vehicle, it must be roadworthy. Again, there is a tendency to skimp on trailer tyres, but if you tow regularly or for long distances, a good set of tyres is essential. Using trailers off road can seriously affect the efficiency of the 4x4, with ground clearance one of the main problems. Military trailers are a good compromise, especially if they are to be towed by an equivalent ex-military vehicle fitted with similar sized wheels.

As an alternative, why not make your own trailer from a kit? These are available from Indespension (see Useful Addresses) who have agents in most areas.

Check the vehicle handbook for any change in tyre pressures that are necessary whilst towing. Make sure that the loading of the trailer is balanced; most of the weight should be located over the axles and not to the front or rear of the trailer.

TOW HITCHES AND TOWING EYES

These come in various sizes and shapes but universally use a 50 mm ball coupling. The ball can be connected directly to the chassis or attached via a drop plate. This allows the height of the tow hitch to

Fig. 7.1 Assortment of different towing eyes – essential for off-road recovery

be adjusted, thus ensuring that the tow bar height and weight is correct for the different trailers. This positioning must be correct to ensure the trailer follows in a straight line and doesn't sway about. When towing a modern lightweight caravan it may be necessary to use a shick-mounted tow ball. The pitching and shock loads can sometimes put unnecessary strain on the caravan chassis, and fitment of this attachment will alleviate the problem. If you are contemplating a military trailer the attachment is via a NATO hitch. This comprises a large hook with a spring-loaded jaw that closes over the top.

It often amazes people to see a tow hitch fitted to the front of an off-road vehicle, but recovery of a stricken vehicle requires a strong attachment point for a rope or cable. The simplest method is a tow ball fitted to the front of the 4x4 but this must be firmly secured with a backing plate if connected to a bumper. One problem with this arrangement is that the tow hitch increases the length of the vehicle. An alternative is to fit two towing eyes or hooks on top of each side of the chassis. The Land Rover D-eyes are large and able to take loops of thick recovery rope. Smaller ones are available that can take shackles and bolts. These can be used to take a solid tow bar

Fig. 7.2 Two different tow hitches. At the top, a NATO hitch for military trailers, at the bottom a standard 50mm ball hitch. Extended drop plates like this should have a stronger

Fig. 7.3 A Dixon-Bate adjustable drop plate for varying the height of the tow hitch. This 50mm ball has an integral claw & pin, an ideal combination

in the form of an 'A' frame. If a disabled vehicle has to be towed long distances off road this towing frame is very effective as the load is being shared by the two sides of the chassis. It is for a similar reason that two eyes or hitches should be used for recovery.

REVERSING A TRAILER

First of all make sure that there is nothing in the way of the trailer, particularly animals or children. Start with the vehicle and trailer in a straight line. Some trailers have a reversing catch which prevents the over-run brakes from operating whilst going backwards. Check that this is engaged. Other trailers with over-run braking will do this automatically.

137

Fig. 7.4 A towing 'A'-frame fitted to eyes on the front of a Land Rover

As you slowly begin to reverse the trailer, apply the opposite steering lock to the direction of the turn you wish to make. The back of the vehicle moves in the opposite way but will set the trailer going on the correct course. This manoeuvre must not be prolonged or the trailer will just jack-knife. Once the trailer is moving correctly, the vehicle must be straightened. Reverse the lock on the steering to the normal position and this should guide the outfit through the rest of the turn. Just keep an eye on the trailer and be prepared to reverse the lock again if it starts to deviate.

Before you attempt to drive forward remember to disengage the reversing catch unless you have an automatic system. Automatic over-run brakes work on the principle that as the weight of the vehicle pushes into the tow bar a lever or hydraulic system applies the brakes proportionally.

The standard door or wing mirrors on most 4x4s will be sufficient for low trailers. For those trailers that are especially wide or high, it is essential to fit mirror extensions so that good visibility can be obtained down both sides.

TOWING HEAVY LOADS

This can place considerable strain on a vehicle's transmission when starting off, especially on slopes. Use low range gears to achieve a smooth and safe start. Begin with either first or second gear and change up to increase the speed up to about 15 mph. Then depress the clutch and bring the transfer lever into neutral. Wait a few seconds, to allow the revs to decrease slightly, before continuing the transfer up into high range. Then immediately select a gear suitable for the speed that you are travelling at and release the clutch. For some vehicles it may be necessary, first of all, to place the main gear lever into neutral before attempting the transfer from low to high range. If you have an automatic transmission this is also necessary but check with your vehicle handbook for the precise details.

8

Off-Road Motor Sport

For many people off roading is simply a means to an end, either for their jobs or as a way to see wild and remote regions. But a good number of people enjoy off roading as a sport, both as spectators and competitors. On-road competition sports demand expensive machinery to get the adrenalin pumping, since high speeds are normally required. For the off-road enthusiast, however, there is everything from sedate rallies where individuals show off their carefully-restored classics to mudslinging safari races of modified half-breeds. Between the two extremes there is the popular trialling that anyone with a 4x4 can enter. None of these off-road motor sports need adversely affect your pocket as your family 4x4 can be entered in non-damaging events. And here you compete on your own terms for the sheer fun of it!

OFF-ROAD CLUBS

If you have any interest at all in these off-road sports then you should join a club. The All-Wheel Drive Club (AWDC) has to be the first to consider. They are the biggest and best organised club and offer a variety of competitive events. They allow just about any vehicle to be used: from a 16-ton, eight-wheel drive monster to a small engined home-made hybrid. For the various competitions they have different classes. All classes follow strict safety guidelines and all events are run under the Royal Automobile Club Blue Book rules. In fact, the AWDC tend to set the standards from which the many other clubs take their lead. If you join the AWDC a bi-monthly publication, *All-Wheel Driver*, is sent to you; each year, too, a yearbook is published. These give details of the events that are going on around the country, plus competition regulations.

Fig. 8.1 A typical AWDC meeting with a variety of machines

Besides the AWDC there are a large number of various 'one make clubs'. For example, the Rhino Club caters for Suzuki drivers. There is a Mitsubishi Owners' Club and a wealth of area groups for the Association of Rover Clubs. In addition, there are even 'one model clubs' such as the Land Rover Series One Club, Series Two Club, 101 Club and Range Rover Register.

There is bound to be a club somewhere to suit your needs. (See Useful Addresses.)

All competitions and events need marshals and the clubs always need volunteers for this role, helping run the trials and safaris. Marshals are needed on the various courses laid out for the competitors, for anything from recording defaults to helping de-bog stuck vehicles. It is an ideal opportunity for you to become involved before actually competing, by watching and learning. Many marshals do not compete because they say the best fun is sorting out the problems on the track, especially during speed events.

There may be opportunities to use your off-road vehicle at other times not connected with motor sport. Quite often clubs in remoter parts of the country offer organised vehicle use in emergencies. For

Fig. 8.2 Trialling: a sport for everyone

example, off roaders have helped to move St John Ambulance personnel. Elsewhere in hill country, the old and infirm may experience problems, especially in winter, travelling to and from isolated cottages at the ends of tracks. Clubs have members who can help in these situations; so, if you join, it will enable you not only to use and enjoy your vehicle off road but to help other people in the process.

It is also good to see some clubs taking a responsible attitude toward the environment, which they could so easily damage. Off roaders can join with local conservation groups, assisting them in getting personnel and equipment into difficult localities. There, too, off roaders can lend both their labour and their vehicles for tasks such as scrub clearance. Your 4x4 is a specialist piece of machinery and it is surprising how many other groups and associations would be interested in your help - and you get to use your vehicle where you want to: off road!

For those drivers with more obscure 4x4 vehicles a club can be vital to maintain a connection with others, to share similar problems and to obtain help from the manufacturer.

TRIALLING

Entering a trial is not for those of an over-competitive nature, because you will probably end up bending your motor and that is unnecessary. Trialling should be for fun.

There are several categories and they vary from club to club. Many clubs hold a Road Tax Vehicle (RTV) trial. It requires no modification to your vehicle and therefore no expense other than the small entrance fee. Your vehicle must be roadworthy - which is then classified as off-roadworthy - and tyres need to be good otherwise problems are likely.

Other trials events can include vehicles that have been modified in some way and do vary in their degree of difficulty.

In all RTV trials the idea is that they should be non-damaging to vehicles. Anyone can enter and it is expertise off road that is under test, not speed. Therefore, there is no timing and you can take as long as you like provided you do not stop. The trial will generally be organised so that between eight and ten sections must be covered. Each is dealt with separately and divided up into ten gates. These

gates are marked with a pair of canes which you drive between. They are numbered in decreasing order from 10 down to 1. Starting with gate 10 the aim is to pass through all gates without stopping or touching a cane. If you do touch or stop then the last gate you entered will be your score. Nil points constitutes a clear round. At the end of the day the scores are totalled and the competitor with the lowest wins.

Drivers' skills are tested on crossing water, muddy terrain, loose surfaces, tight turns, slippery banks and steep hills, but the obstacles themselves will depend on the location and the organisers' ingenuity. If a section looks difficult and a particularly tricky part approaches do not be frightened to back off and retire. You are there for the fun of it, after all! People do get caught up in the trap of thinking they have to do it, swept along on a tide of competitiveness. So, it is worth taking stock of your potential, very carefully!

There are also husband and wife classes which make for a good day out with the family and, for pushing your expertise to the limit, the AWDC and other clubs run night trials. Night off roading adds a completely new dimension to what may at first appear to be a rather simple route. Depending on the event they may operate from seven in the evening to midnight or even three in the morning.

RACING

These events are termed 'safaris' and involve racing against the clock over very rough and demanding terrain. They are organised by a number of off-road clubs and the different classes are determined by the power of the vehicles taking part.

Safaris attract some very imaginative and ingenious designs. Most are based on the standard 4x4 chassis although VW Buggies are a common sight. The latter are a cheap way into off-road racing and they are often seen for sale through the off-road press.

Safari competitions have very stringent safety rules - indeed, they have to. Whatever the modifications to the machine it must have a full roll cage built to a very high specification. Modern crash helmets

Illustrations, facing page:
Fig. 8.3 Trialling: The Good, the 'Pad' and the Ugly!

*Fig. 8.4 A hybridised vehicle being used in a Safari Championship
(Courtesy of Justyn Willsmore)*

must be worn, along with a proper, full harness belt. Any components that project from the engine must be protected by guards. These are the basic safety rules; the clubs publish more detailed regulations and specifications and it is therefore advisable to make contact with the club scrutineer or the RAC Chief Officer when you enter your name.

Safari races generate plenty of adrenalin for drivers and bystanders alike. The circuits are about 4 to 5 miles round, with competitors driving up to ten runs for each event. Some seem to be arranged in a sea of mud and even if your intention is purely to go and watch it is just as well to take a 4x4 to reach the car park! Venues are arranged in most parts of the country and a good many of the larger ones are set up on army training areas such as Bovington and Sidbury.

Off-road racing may not attract the media attention which some other motor sports do, but it is well organised and venues are efficiently run, with computer timing and the electronic display of results often to be seen.

SHOW RALLIES

This is the gentle pursuit of the off roader and not to be confused with speed rallying. Organised by the 'one make clubs' these rallies are where enthusiasts show off their meticulously restored classics. One could say they are for those who do not want to get their vehicles covered in mud. Much of the day is spent talking about the displays and, being so peaceful, they are a very different aspect of off-road sport.

For example, the Military Vehicle Trust has meetings for those interested in 4x4 military and larger vehicles. The Trust caters for static displays, but also has trials to demonstrate the equipment. There are even rallies and camp gatherings to such venues as Normandy, to see the D-Day beaches. As with many of these types of club they can help the individual enthusiast with restoration work by giving advice and assistance in obtaining parts.

9

Expeditions and Travel

Off roading and expedition travel are almost synonymous. The opportunities for independent travel are limitless and many people purchase a 4x4 for that reason. It could be a camping holiday for the family, a trek for a group of young adventurers or a major expedition to central Africa. Many miss out on this ultimate off-roading experience because of their lack of confidence. Hopefully, this chapter will help to dispel some of their doubts and tempt them to travel further afield. Remote and beautiful areas still exist, waiting to be discovered, and are within driving distance for the family holiday. In Chapter 10 there is a brief summary of some of these places, where off-roading potential can be exploited. Whether you hope to travel through the mountain tracks of the Pyrenees or go overland to India, there should be something in this section of the book to speed your passage.

The rugged, go-anywhere character of the 4x4, together with its ability to carry heavy loads, make it the ideal vehicle for this type of journey. But the prospective traveller should give careful consideration to choosing the right vehicle for the job and preparing and/or modifying that vehicle. (The choice of vehicle may of course, be a foregone conclusion!)

CHOOSING A VEHICLE

Many factors will influence your choice of vehicle, none more so than availability of funds! There are, too, some other important considerations.

Country
Find out from the tourist board or embassy of the country in which the trip is to be based or through which you will travel whether there

Fig. 9.1 Two very different expeditions. Above: a diesel turbo Land Rover equipped for the Sulawesi Camel Trophy. Below: following the 'Jeep' tracks that cross the Picos de Europa, North Spain

are restrictions or potential problems. Importation of your vehicle into certain countries may incur taxes specific to types, number of seats and engines. For example, Icelandic customs usually tax diesel engines.

Petrol or diesel?

Diesel prices on the Continent are significantly lower than in the United Kingdom. Therefore the advantages or otherwise of choosing a diesel or petrol driven vehicle need careful consideration and comparison. In addition, you may wish to take into account the benefit to the environment of using a vehicle that can run on lead-free petrol. Further information is given in Chapter 2, pages 53-54.

Diesel advantages
- A cheaper fuel
- More miles to the gallon
- Widely available
- No electrics to flood when wading in rivers
- Easier to maintain, no electrics to go wrong
- Low fire risk

Diesel disadvantages
- Noisy engine which can be irritating on long journeys unless carefully sound proofed
- Lower cruising speeds
- Contamination (e.g. water) will cause more problems than petrol

Petrol advantages
- Faster cruising speeds
- Cleaner
- Engines often better understood than diesel ones

Petrol disadvantages
- Expensive, except in countries self-sufficient in fuel (where it is about the same cost as diesel)
- Highly inflammable
- Fewer miles per gallon (so more has to be carried)

Availability of spares
One thinks of Land Rovers as being universally available, but for political reasons some countries do not import them. South America is one place where having a jeep is preferable. Toyota and Nissan are found throughout the world; Toyota especially, whose early Land Cruisers are commonplace.

It can be difficult finding Land Rover spares in France but neighbouring Spain has a Land Rover/Santana dealer in every major town. Land Rovers in North Africa and the Sahara are still a common sight but most are Series Two and Three vehicles. Spares, new and secondhand, are found fairly easily and if not can usually be made or repaired by the skilful Arab mechanics. For example, in Morocco, in cases where we would buy a new solenoid, the mechanic is likely to break the sealed unit open, repair and glue it back together again. In Third World countries it pays to have a relatively uncomplicated engine. Scrap-yards with occasional 4x4 wrecks can be found in the most unlikely places.

Load-carrying capacity
Overloaded vehicles will not perform well off road and may be downright dangerous. It is better to opt for a larger vehicle; for instance, a long wheelbase Land Rover instead of a short one. Trailers will increase the payload but may considerably reduce off-road potential. Ex-military box trailers are designed to be towed by Land Rovers, using the same wheels, and are a good compromise.

BEST BUYS

Some of the FWD off-road vehicles available were described in Chapter Two. Each has its own virtues and vices which makes choosing difficult. The final decision will probably be a compromise. It may be that you will find FWD unnecessary for your purposes. Anyone who has travelled on North African dirt tracks will vouch for the number of Citroen 2CVs, Peugeot 504s and Renault 4s that continually overtake the fuel-guzzling Land Rover, and if you travel off road along the difficult mountain tracks of the Spanish Pyrenees you will invariably find a Fiat 500 at the end of the track!

One of the advantages of taking your own vehicle is the storage space available to carry all those little luxuries which make it a home-from-home. Cars rarely have enough space. But, more importantly, whether crossing Iceland's interior or the sands of the Tanezrouft in the Sahara, your chosen vehicle will have to be able to carry extra fuel as well as supplies of food and water.

The final choice of vehicle has to be based on the terrain to be crossed and the load to be carried. It is essential, therefore, that areas of a country which lack fuel supplies are identified and the volume of fuel to be carried calculated.

Remember that fuel consumption will be high in rough terrain and that prolonged use of low range gears may halve the normal mpg. Once calculated, add 30 per cent to allow for deviations, mis-navigation, lack of fuel at the estimated refuelling sites and for the extra consumption that just de-bogging a stuck vehicle will take. Remember also, that a 5-gallon jerrycan not only takes up a lot of valuable space but weighs 55 lb when full.

When going to purchase a vehicle for expedition use there is always the gambler's option: buy a cheap but basically sound vehicle that requires a degree of rebuilding. Time will be the greatest necessity, for once parts are disturbed it can upset the balance of other components. Still, there is nothing like taking a vehicle apart to learn how it works. Bear in mind that one always finds twice as much wrong with the vehicle with this approach. Allow for this in the expedition budget.

Volkswagen Combi

A Volkswagen Combi van-cum-caravanette may be the best compromise. They have more interior space than a Land Rover, are cheaper to run, more comfortable to live and sleep in and spares can be found almost anywhere in the world. Air-cooling for the engine dispenses with possible radiator and hose problems and they have reasonable ground clearance. The weight of the engine is directly above the drive wheels and the independent suspension, as well as being tough, gives good wheel articulation. Off road they perform extremely well, as long as their limitations are taken into consideration and they are treated with care. For example, avoid loading the front of the vehicle and/or the roof. In addition, the cooling system is designed to operate with the engine door shut: do not be tempted to leave it open for extra cooling. The 2-litre engine is preferable to the standard 1.6-litre for crossing sand but either will provide excellent expedition service. The FWD version of the latest Transporter series was introduced in 1985, making this vehicle even more tempting.

Chevrolet Blazer
American vehicles, as a rule, consume too much fuel and outside
the Americas will give headaches in obtaining spares. The Chevrolet
Blazer with its live axles, part-time FWD and coil springs is a
possibility, however, and is in many respects similar to the Range
Rover.

Range Rover
Range Rovers may be the ultimate in expedition go-anywhere luxury
but, despite their hulk, they are poor load carriers, and fuel
consumption may be a problem if you have to carry petrol across
the Sahara. In the latter respect the Turbo Diesel version would be
preferable. The price new is the same as the petrol version, but
secondhand the diesel version holds a higher value. It may therefore
prove rather more expensive to buy than the petrol version. A diesel
conversion could be a good alternative as it is an excellent and
comfortable touring machine. Jerrycans fit very neatly in the rear
luggage section, and high quality expedition roof racks are available.
An uprated suspension would be essential in this instance.

Land Rover
Land Rovers provide the greatest range of choices, both in size and
engine types. This choice is widened still further by considering the
number of ex-military models that can be purchased through
selected dealers. Land Rovers have to be the choice of vehicle for
expeditions. Short wheelbase forms are most versatile off road but
the long wheelbase has a greater load-carrying capacity and is easier
to live/sleep inside. This type can be bought in either the three-door
hard top or five-door safari models. The former is a cheaper option
and the back can be laid out as comfortable living accommodation.
It is also more secure. Ex-army hard and soft top long wheelbase
versions are widely available. They can be excellent buys and
usually have, as standard, many facilities you may later want to use,
e.g. oil coolers and heavy-duty suspension. Those in ambulance
guise have a substantial hard top and, occasionally, air conditioning.
They make ideal camper vehicles with a high carrying capacity and
good security. Ambulances usually have a low mileage and have
not worked so hard as most military machines. Ex-army ambulance
Land Rovers have plenty of space but with their large and heavy
body modification they can be rather unwieldy off road. However,
the ex-military forward-control 101 Land Rover is an ideal expedition
vehicle. With the potential for more interior space it can carry a ton

Fig. 9.2   101 forward-control Land Rover. A tough expedition contender with basically Range Rover parts

comfortably. The basic shell can be purchased and built to your specification in seating, hard/soft top and engine. The standard vehicle uses the Range Rover engine and transmission plus heavy-duty Salisbury axles front and rear.

People are put off by the possible hard life that the military vehicle would have been put through – certainly some have been regularly dropped from a helicopter, so inspect the chassis carefully – but there are ex-army vehicles with very low mileage on the clock, as they have been kept in storage. Thus a Series 3 Land Rover could fetch a relatively high price but require less preparation.

The Series Three ex-army Land Rovers are all four-cylinder petrol driven with most parts as standard. However, some spares will be different, e.g the water pump and exhaust: the former simply has a different number of holes but the exhaust is very different (and better, as it goes through the chassis). Two (long range) fuel tanks are located under the front seats. They are switched into use whilst driving, using a brass lever near the driver's legs. The fact that there is no external filler cap for the fuel tank is good security. Some ex-military vehicles may have a normal fuel tank but are slow to fill. They are, however, explosion-proof.

Because of the diverse uses to which Land Rovers have been put, many weird and wonderful types are available secondhand. Watch out for ex-gas and electricity board auctions (usually advertised in *Exchange and Mart*). Ex-water authority vehicles, too, usually become available after about eight years and have low mileages. They are normally basic models but may come with heavy-duty winches or body modifications Those fitted with accessories like winches may have low mileages but still have worked hard all their lives. The engines would have worked all day despite the vehicle remaining static. Some have 'workrooms' built on to a pickup chassis, making a purpose-built, cheaply-priced caravanette. Watch out for the adverts!

Of all the engines possible the four-cylinder 2.25-litre petrol engine has been well tried and tested by thousands of Land Rover users over the years. As well as being very reliable the spares should be easily available. The six-cylinder 2.6-litre petrol engine can give more problems than the extra power warrants. Abroad, they are not very common and spares are not so easily found. On top of that, the mechanical fuel pump of the 2.25 is easier to repair than the electrical one of the 2.6, and the bigger engine is less efficient in the heat. The V8 found in the later Series Three and in the 110 and the 90, however, can give effortless cruising and reduce driving strain (so prevalent in a Land Rover driver!) It is a very different engine. The low down torque makes plugging through sand dunes comparatively easy and fuel consumption is not necessarily that far removed from the other petrol engines, particularly when towing or carrying a heavy load.

The earlier 2.25 diesel engine was reliable though incredibly under-powered when driving on tarmac roads. Perhaps the biggest problem with this diesel is the problem in actually finding one with a suitable body. The 2.5 diesel engine in the 110 and the 90 series was something of an improvement but the turbocharged version now makes it a more acceptable performer.

There are adverts in the 4x4 press for vehicles already prepared for an expedition. One should check these very thoroughly if they have just returned from a trip, checking especially for non-standard components. Fuel pumps are a commonly 'bodged' part.

Umm Alter
Originally made in France as the Cournil, the UMM is a fairly basic and uncomplicated vehicle. It is gaining popularity in the UK as a sturdy and competent off-roader. Few recorded expeditions have used the UMM.

Available with the long wheelbase it has an excellent carrying capacity and the standard Peugeot engine not only gives a good performance but should not present too many problems with spares.

Volvo Laplander
The Volvo Laplander, although no longer produced, is seen in a surprising number of places both in the United Kingdom and abroad. Often they have been converted into superb caravanettes and, with the 3/4-ton capacity and excellent visibility, this forward control vehicle makes an ideal expedition wagon – but with limited commuter appeal! Powered by the four-cylinder engine of the 200 series car, spares will be restricted in many countries.

The four- or six-wheel versions of the C303 and C304 Volvos are very impressive and reminiscent of the Mercedes Unimog.

Fig. 9.3   The Mercedes Unimog.   A formidable, if expensive, expedition vehicle

Mercedes Unimog

Marginally better fuel consumption than the Volvos and will be seen in most European, African and some Asian off-road regions. Spares are widely available. A complete 'home-from-home' can be built on to the chassis and with the high ground clearance, portal axles and coil suspension it is a real go-anywhere vehicle. It has a high load capacity which is just as well if you have one of the older, petrol versions. All that extra fuel that will be consumed has to be carried somewhere! More recent diesel options are much more efficient. Like the Pingauer, they make excellent but expensive expedition vehicles.

Lada Niva

The erratic distribution of spares abroad makes the Lada Niva a problematic though interesting choice, but its limited load capacity may be a problem.

Japanese vehicles

Generally, the older Japanese vehicles have limited load capacities for major expeditions. The more recent long wheelbase vehicles, with the diesel engine option, do have a much higher capacity. Reliability is excellent. Toyota Land Cruiser stands out as the one Japanese vehicle most likely to be found in Africa (especially East Africa) and Australasia. In many countries they have taken over from Land Rover as the prime off roader. Nissan, Mitsubishi and Isuzu have spread their dealerships considerably in recent years, but it would be advisable to obtain up-to-date information on the availability of spares and location of dealers when planning trips abroad.

WHERE TO BUY

Land Rovers and other FWD vehicles are a specialised commodity. Would-be purchasers should first buy a copy of one of the off-road magazines where specialist dealers advertise. Whether you are interested in up-market sophistication, expedition preparation or ex-military transport, most needs will be catered for here. However, to find the right vehicle may require travelling the length of the country. To help in your search check the local *Autotrader* magazine and, for further afield, *Exchange and Mart* (all available at your newsagents on Thursdays).

Travellers coming from North America to Europe or Africa would be better off purchasing a suitable vehicle in the United Kingdom and selling it before their return. Most off-road vehicles, by virtue of their strength, usually have good re-sale value. Secondhand Land Rovers are especially good in this respect.

Buying a secondhand Land Rover

Whilst a secondhand Land Rover is nearly always a good buy, mistakes can happen. In this section we try to point out areas where problems might be found.

Gearbox and Engine

Check the synchromesh, changing both up and down the box. Decelerate in all gears to make sure the lever does not jump out. Try to pull away in second gear; an unladen vehicle should have little problem. Don't forget to test the transfer box, low range and the FWD. Check for oil leaks around the gearbox, especially around the clutch bell-housing. Oil on the clutch could spell disaster later on.

The engine should be clean of oil and breathing correctly.

Axle casings

Check they are not bent. There is always a degree of play in the differentials but not excessively so. If the chrome on the swivels is heavily pitted, inner hub oil seals are likely to keep breaking.

Rust

Check the rear cross-member of the chassis, below the rear door. Underneath, check the main longitudinal chassis, especially where the springs are mounted, as they could easily break under load. The outriggers are comparatively cheap to buy but labour costs to cut out the old and weld on the new may be the most expensive part. The aluminium body skin will not rust but may show signs of oxidation and corrosion. Door frameworks are of steel and quickly show signs of rust. Replacement Safari rear doors can be found reasonably priced and front doors, up to the later 110 and 90, are in two easily replaced parts. However, to re-glaze the tops is a time-consuming process and needs to be taken into consideration along with other labour-intensive jobs. The middle doors of the Safari 109-in models are one piece and expensive to replace. Welding small plates to the frame around the windows will extend their life.

Suspension
Make sure the leaf springs are intact and that the shape is correct. Bunching in the middle suggests that they are reaching the end of their life. This may not be important if you are going to upgrade to a heavier duty spring. Front spring hangers should be almost vertical and rear hangers at about 45 degrees.

Registration
If you own, or are going to purchase, a secondhand vehicle make sure that the engine number is the same as that in the registration document: FWD vehicles do undergo engine changes, often to suit them to different fuels. This change may not have been recorded in the document and may go unnoticed – until, that is, you arrive at some remote border crossing and the guards decide to check!

VEHICLE PREPARATION

Tyres
New tyres have to be the best bet before any major trip. To keep them in good order, make sure the pressures are checked daily. Heat will increase pressure dramatically. A summer's day in Spain will double the tyre pressure so check they are normal at breakfast time, before the journey starts. There is a temptation to carry two spare wheels (or more!), but an extra wheel adds kilos of weight that could be better used. The extent and duration of the trip will decide the need for more than one spare. If possible, just take an extra tyre. If your journey is going to involve extensive off roading away from possible repairers then you will have to carry out the repair. With some practice it is not difficult. Carry spare inner tubes, a set of tyre levers (which only cost a few pounds), a rubber mallet and repair kit. The latter consists mainly of patches, glue and talcum powder.

The problem may be more than just a puncture; the tyre itself may be damaged. Splits can be stitched with nylon and then glued with Araldite but only in dire emergency. To break the beading between tyre and rim use the high-lift jack. Place the wheel under the bumper and put the base of the jack on the tyre. Jacking against the bumper should break the seal. As an alternative, try to drive over the tyre!

If you are likely to be carrying out your own tyre repairs it will be worth your while, before you go on your travels, to test that it is possible to break the beading on the tyres. For example, some

Range Rover tyres are very difficult. Michelin XYZ tyres are normally 12-ply rated and virtually impossible to change in the field.

Crossing sand requires a lower pressure than the normal. (See page 94.) Note that radial tyres can survive lower pressures than cross-ply. Buying sand tyres (e.g. Michelin XS) can be an advantage but their softer more pliable rubber can easily be damaged on rock. Deserts have more rock and stones than sand so think carefully before any trip as two sets of tyres would have to be carried. For example, the Tarmac road from Algiers southward to Tamanrasset crosses the Sahara and is comparatively 'new'. The road surface tends to break up and the sharp tarmac edges, if hit at any speed above a crawling pace, will cut tyres to shreds.

For reinflation, purchase either a mini-electric compressor to run from the battery (cheap and available from most car accessory shops) or try the spark-plug type. (See also page 67 for other alternatives.)

Suspension

Loading a vehicle with the necessary accoutrement will inevitably change its handling characteristics. This can be improved by changing the shock absorbers or suspension, although on many vehicles you will have little chance of changing the suspension.

Land Rovers with leaf springs have a choice of normal, heavy-duty or 1-ton. This does not necessarily mean you can increase the payload but it will improve cornering and ride when loaded. A set of laden standard leaf springs will wear very fast when used extensively off road; they will have to be changed every other year. The 1-ton springs go on for years, although the ride when empty can be most uncomfortable. Heavy-duty springs are a good compromise.

Overloading

Even with the best suspension and shock absorber system, overloading can cause major problems. Therefore careful thought and planning must go into the arrangement of heavy loads. Fluids such as fuel and water are rarely given the consideration they need, being a rather transient item. It is only when you fill up with these that their presence is felt. Try to fit all permanent loads as low as possible in the vehicle to keep the centre of gravity down. Long-range fuel tanks are an excellent substitute for jerrycans which invariably end up on the roof. They attach to the chassis and so keep

Fig. 9.4 A 110 Land Rover high capacity pickup, modified by Peter and Ida Kirsten for desert use. Water tanks are located low down, below the shower which is attached to the side. Notice the PSP fixed to the roof

the weight in the correct place. Water tanks can also be fitted in similar positions.

Land Rovers are the most versatile vehicles to which such equipment can be added but fitting an extra 10-gallon tank necessitates the loss of the very useful tool box under the front passenger seat. Secondhand long-range fuel tanks can be obtained from scrapyards dealing in ex-army Land Rovers. These have them fitted as standard.

North Africa is the place to see a range of vehicle conversions. All modifications are designed to reduce overloading but retain versatility. Limited only by people's imaginations, off-road and travel instincts combine to personalise vehicles, giving them creature comforts and adaptability. Lightweight alloys and strong plastics enable some amazing hybrids to develop (see Fig. 9.4).

Roof racks

Roof racks have been much maligned in the past, because once fitted you may be tempted to overload them. If you intend to cross large

Fig. 9.5 A heavy duty, reinforced Brownchurch roof rack that is suitable for aluminium guttering. Notice the vertical supports

areas of sand, such as in the Sahara, weighted roof racks can affect the efficiency of sand tyres, increasing the chance of becoming bogged. However, as long as this is borne in mind they can be a valuable accessory. When buying you should pay attention to the method of attachment, the construction and size.

Bolt-on types can be more stable but are limited to certain vehicles. Box section is much better than tubular, but galvanised steel is essential, otherwise rust establishes itself very quickly. A body-length rack which is supported off the wings or bumper should be avoided; firstly because visibility on slope descents is severely restricted, and secondly because carrying heavy weights such as jerrycans above the cab is not a good idea as the weight is in the wrong place. However, the type of roof rack attached at the front by braces to the windscreen hinge brackets can be used for lightweight items and can be useful in reducing sun glare on the windscreen. Overloaded roof racks can crack windscreens if not supported in this manner. There are some very good heavy-duty expedition roof racks with reinforced brackets at the corners. (See Brownchurch in Useful Addresses.) Late 90 or 110 Land Rovers have an aluminium roof gutter, so ensure that the correct model of roof rack is purchased.

A ladder at the rear can also be a valuable addition.

Jerrycans

Many people use the roof rack to carry jerrycans for both fuel and water. The suspension is designed to take the greatest weight at the rear and so cans must be positioned at the rear of the roof rack, over the wheels. A roof rack can be suitably modified to carry eight, 5-gallon steel cans (see Fig. 9.9). The bar that swings over the top can be padlocked for security. The jerrycans can be filled in place and their contents transferred by siphoning. This reduces the need to move the cans, which is useful in a hot country where full cans will heat up in the day to become well and truly jammed.

New jerrycans are expensive but good secondhand ones can be bought through the companies that deal with ex-military vehicles. Before buying them test for leakages with a small amount of fuel. Watch out for the American cans; they have a screw cap and are inferior, mainly because they are useless at pouring.

New, plastic jerrycans can be used for water.

Tarpaulins

Tarpaulins can be obtained in different sizes to cover baggage but purpose-designed ones can be produced by sailmakers. They are constructed as two open-box sections with the four corners heat welded. One is placed on to the roof rack and baggage loaded into it. The second box acts as the top, being placed upside down over the other with the sides between the bottom box and the edges of the rack. Brass eyes set at intervals into the edge of this top box can be used to rope the entire structure down.

Large roof racks can be used as sleeping quarters and there are some excellent (if rather expensive) roof tents available (see Fig. 9.6).

Fire hazard

When filling up from jerrycans the static build-up in a vehicle can jump to the can causing it to catch fire. Burnt-out vehicles are seen in remote areas where cans have to be used. It does depend on a charge from the vehicle and this varies considerably from situation to situation. A safe way to overcome the problem is to have a clip lead from the vehicle to the can and operator, thus equalising the static charge throughout. A lead to earth may help but in very dry conditions it is not always reliable.

Fig. 9.6   A typical roof tent on an Italian Land Rover

Extra battery and split charging

The more you modify your vehicle for expedition work the more connections – and therefore demands — are made on the battery. A winch can kill the battery in minutes if it is not operated correctly. Campers' fluorescent lights will use less electricity and are a safe option but long-term use in a camp can have its effect, as can the operation of water pumps. Battery cells can, of course, suddenly give at any time. Ultimately you may be faced with a battery crisis and inevitably this will be in some remote corner of the world with no other vehicle in sight.

A spare battery is a good option, but finding a suitable place to store it may be a problem. If it is located near other stored items it is essential that some form of insulating cover is placed over the top to prevent shorting across the terminals. A quick-fit, plastic box terminal is now available which overcomes this problem. Make sure the battery is secure; elastic luggage straps can be used to hold it down in the boot.

A number of split chargers, some very sophisticated, are available to maintain the battery charge. Caravan and camping dealers carry a number of makes but there are some inexpensive and very simple systems. While you drive, the charge is sustained in your second battery without affecting the first. It is important that the two batteries should be charged independently by the alternator and that they are isolated so that one cannot drain into the other. Auxiliary equipment, like the winch, fridge and extra lighting, should be connected to the second battery.

Always carry a set of heavy-duty jump leads. Even if you do not need them there is a good chance that you will meet someone else who does.

Bull bars and light guards

Light clusters on vehicles are expensive to replace. Most off roaders will find it useful to protect lights with either grills or large bull bars. In many countries, driving with a damaged light is considered a traffic offence, and many continental countries make it a legal obligation to carry spare light bulbs or sealed beams. Light grills or plastic protectors will protect from flying stones as well as vegetation.

Fig. 9.7   The ultimate in protection. The ARB roo-bar and bumper with fitted Warn Winch. The front underside is protected with Southdown Engineering skidplates

Fig. 9.8   The Kirsten bumper – an alternative to a bull bar. It is particularly suited for driving in long grass to keep seed heads free from the radiator. Reduces approach angle

Bull bars look more macho but although they can protect bodywork from boulders and trees they do not always help to protect lights from small objects. If you are looking to buy bull bars, consider those with built-in grills for the lights rather than those only designed solely for looks and poser value. Bull bars are only as strong as their connection to the vehicle: make sure that the ones you buy have very solid fixings and attach them to the bumper or chassis with as many bolts as possible. One bolt at either end is asking for trouble. If the bar takes a knock it will just be pushed back on to the radiator grill or wing, causing the damage it was put there to protect against. Do not tow from a bull bar. Make sure you can get through any grills or bars to wash the headlights. It is now possible to buy bars with hinged grills to give rapid access to the lights.

There are very good Australian-made bull or 'roo' bars with reinforced bumper and winch mount, now available in the United Kingdom from David Bowyer's Off Road Centre (see Useful Addresses).

Warning triangles

To carry these is a legal obligation in most countries. What is not often realised is that two should be carried if your vehicle is capable of seating more than nine people. This does not mean that by removing a set of seats rules governing that type of vehicle are automatically void; it may depend on the recommendations of the manufacturer and what the log book or registration document states.

SECURITY

Whilst travelling across the Mediterranean on a ferry bound for Morocco we saw, for the first time, what we took to be security paranoia from other expedition groups who had previously travelled to the 'dark continent'. This was our first visit but we were confident of our security arrangements. All three of our long-wheelbase Safari Land Rovers had good locks and the rear sections were boxed internally with wire mesh. At night people slept inside the vehicles. And it was on the first night that we were robbed of over £2,500 worth of cheques, money and goods. The 'decent' chaps did leave our passports behind, but we learnt from this experience that security could never be too high.

When travelling abroad there is always this concern with possible break-ins or even having the vehicle itself stolen, and the problem is heightened in many Third World countries (although one look at an off-road vehicle in Italy, festooned with padlocks, shows the problem is just as great in parts of Europe). Prevention is always best, so try to avoid leaving the vehicle unattended in back streets or on the edges of towns. Keep it out in the open.

In Third World countries you may not pay car park fees but you may find it beneficial to pay a boy to look after the vehicle. Some North African cities do employ officials (usually men with a cap and stick) who you should pay to guard over your possessions. Campsites, too, are patrolled by armed guards to stop thieves, so use them where you can.

Fig. 9.9   The ex-army Land Rover to the left is carrying the spare fuel and equipment for the group. Note the line up of jerry cans at the back of the modified roof rack. The bar locks in place. Five ex-ammunition boxes have been bolted to the rack and contain vehicle and medical spares. They are painted white to reflect heat and have a padlocked bar to secure the lids

Storing valuables

Vehicles with a soft top are very pleasant in the heat but can be a security risk. In this instance you may consider putting all valuables in locked boxes bolted to the vehicle. If you do not spend time in towns and cities and stay in the countryside you are far less likely to be robbed.

Storing equipment on roof racks can be a problem, so if you must put valuable items up top put them in ammunition boxes which are then bolted down to the rack. You will need numerous padlocks. Buy lengths of chain to secure the spare wheels and jerrycans. Some roof racks have a moveable bar which can be padlocked to secure jerrycans. If you transfer the cans to the rear of the roof rack it is advisable to transfer the bar as well.

Expensive off-road vehicles have a security box fitted as standard. These strong boxes can be purchased separately and bolted to the inside of the vehicle in an inconspicuous place. As long as you fit a strong lock it is quite easy to make up your own version. The boxes are ideal for carrying important travel documents, passports and money. You may consider two security boxes, one of which is well out of sight and welded to the chassis. This box is the one containing the absolute essentials for when the first box is found and broken open. The chances are the thieves will not look for a second box.

Door locks

They can be broken to gain entrance. On an older vehicle you should think of fitting a simple but effective hasp, staple and padlock. Valuable vehicles can be fitted with any one of the many security alarms available. The important feature is that they should sound the vehicle horn or a siren to deter the would-be thief from continuing his efforts. Some alarms work on a pendulum system that operates the siren when the vehicle is rocked from side to side; perhaps a good idea in Third World countries where a vehicle can become a climbing frame for the local children. Other good gadgets include those that send out infra-red waves to pick up movement inside, even hands passing through windows, and pressure pads that are placed below the floor mats to set off the alarm when trodden on.

Windscreens

Those held in place by rubber mouldings (most modern vehicles) are a potential access point. Thieves can easily cut round the rubber with a modelling knife and push the glass in. A good cure for this problem is windscreen security conversion by Overland Ltd, which consists of a set of steel strips pop riveted to the window frame, overlapping the rubber. (See Useful Addresses.)

EXTRAS TO CONSIDER

Macho types may consider extras unnecessary, but one should consider them if only as a means of reducing driver fatigue, especially on long journeys abroad.

Sound proofing and carpeting
Journeys can be greatly improved by fitting a combined carpet/sound proofing kit to the interior of the cab.

Overdrive units
These can be expensive to fit but considerably improve long motorway journeys by reducing engine revs. Overdrives will also improve fuel consumption and reduce engine wear. They are a great asset and are consequently highly sought after. It can be very difficult to track down a secondhand unit.

'Lumenition'
This reduces problems with the electrics, gives better starting from cold, and may also improve fuel consumption. You should use the types that allow retention of the original electrics, namely the points, so if the system fails you have a back-up.

Shortwave radio
You may wish to get away from what is happening in the world, but listening to the BBC World Service could be helpful if you are entering a sensitive area, whether it be a war zone or one experiencing flooding.

CB radio
Though limited to your immediate location, if several vehicles are travelling in convoy CB radios are almost essential. In convoy on long journeys CB can assist morale as well as preventing numerous stops for route discussions. When crossing difficult terrain the leader can keep everyone informed of what is happening up front. Most officials of the world turn a blind eye to CB radios fitted in a

vehicle – even neurotic police in the Sahara normally ignore them. However, do not flaunt them in sensitive places and keep their use to essentials. Buying secondhand from a reputable dealer will produce a bargain and the dealer can recommend a good aerial.

Floorspace
The rear bench seats can be removed from long wheelbase vehicles and a tough wire grill fitted across the interior to separate the back from the front like a 'dog guard'. The back can then be packed to prevent gear flying about when the vehicle is tackling slopes or when braking. In addition, it gives reasonable security as access is only from the rear door. Selected artefacts can be fitted to the grill, e.g. a fire extinguisher.

Floodlights
A single floodlight fitted to the rear can be useful when reversing off road at night. It is invaluable, too, when erecting tents or helping with engine problems on another vehicle. A ploughing work light has a wide beam, swivels on its base and has a plastic stone guard that clips on to glass.

Seating
Vinyl seats can make travelling in a hot climate most uncomfortable. A simple solution is to take some old sheets to drape over the seats. Alternatively, a towelling material can be used to make seat covers. The benefits are enormous. A further alternative is to replace them with non-standard cloth seats obtained from a scrap-yard. Beaded seat covers will keep you cooler in a hot climate.

Insect netting
If you intend to travel in tundra regions (e.g. Lapland), or in parts of the tropics where malaria-carrying mosquitoes are abundant, do fit netting. In such regions it is an essential rather than a luxury. Use heavy-duty mosquito netting which is relatively stiff. Cut it out to fit the areas of window openings and then the edges can be attached by thin strips of aluminium, screwed down into the frame.

Fans & Air conditioning
A 12V oscillating fan for the dashboard can be a great comfort in the heat. They can be purchased from heavy goods accessory shops. Likewise, diesel cab heaters can be fitted for cold comfort. These are good for passengers, but not always for the vehicle. Power is

needed for a compressor, using up extra fuel. Such machinery tends to be complicated.

Satellite Navigation

For any form of travel a compass is essential equipment. During the 1980s American technology came to the fore and gave us a rather cumbersome and expensive Transit system of navigation that employed five orbiting satellites. With the system it was possible to produce a longitude and latitude fix to within an accuracy of around 300 metres. The latest system, GPS (Global Positioning System) uses twenty-four satellites to yield a very accurate, virtually instantaneous, three dimensional location. Best of all, it is so compact that it can easily be held in the palm of the hand. The built-in antenna will give a position anywhere in the world to a matter of metres, providing longitude, latitude and altitude with just a few touches of the buttons. There are several models to choose from; the Sony Pyxis is particularly versatile with a swivel, cylindrical aerial. It can be powered either from the vehicle's battery or from its own dry cells. The GPS units should be within the budgets of most expeditions and can be obtained from ElectroTech. (See Useful Addresses.)

INSURANCE & DOCUMENTS

The best laid plans can always go awry. Once abroad and the further you travel into the remote areas the more expensive it becomes to sort out problems of health, lost or stolen belongings and vehicles. Thus carefully organised insurance has to be at the top of your list of preparations.

A starting point is to apply to your local DHSS office to obtain an E111 form for health cover whilst travelling in any of the EEC countries. This gives basic cover, but is not comprehensive and it is worth taking out additional cover. Some countries, such as those in Scandinavia, have special arrangements with the United Kingdom to help with health problems abroad but it will still cost you money. Normally the policy you take out to cover health will also cover your belongings but look at the small print to see the maximum they will pay per item. As this can be quite low it is important to have expensive cameras and similar valuables insured separately. Equipment carried on roof racks is not usually covered on travel insurance; check also whether there is an exclusion clause on camping equipment. (See Fennell Turner and Taylor Limited in Useful Addresses if you have a problem with the latter.) If you have any baggage stolen when abroad make sure that a note is obtained from a nearby police station, otherwise you could have problems when making a claim.

Many off-road enthusiasts may feel that taking out a policy covering roadside assistance is unnecessary. However, such policies do include a recovery scheme to bring the vehicle home. This is important because when you enter a country on holiday there is an agreement whereby your vehicle and equipment is allowed in for a limited period. In some countries, e.g. Iceland, the date you intend to leave is written on to a sticker by a customs officer and attached to the windscreen (and does not come off!)

Most Third World countries enter such details in your passport. This means that even if your beloved vehicle catches fire or is written off in an accident and has to be dumped you will be liable to pay import duty to the country concerned. Insurance will cover this eventuality.

For most continental travel, hunt around the different insurance schemes to find the one best suited to your requirements. The RAC and the AA provide packages for motorists, but so do most of the big insurance companies such as Norwich Union and General Accident. Check the proposal forms carefully for what is covered. On the whole most companies' proposals are very similar, but one difference is the length of time that the policy covers. The AA normally run their 5-Star Insurance Policy for 31 days, so if you intend to be away for only a fortnight then a General Accident policy may save a surprising amount. Most companies have a tendency to use Europ Assistance to provide vehicle cover. The AA 5-Star policy now includes North Africa.

When driving your vehicle in the EEC you will retain third party cover without any additional premium. However, to maintain your comprehensive insurance you need to take out a green card, issued by your own insurance company. This card is mandatory for all other countries. Outside Europe this insurance will not be comprehensive and can become costly. Third party insurance can be purchased when crossing the borders of most African countries.

For travel in Africa and some other continents a Carnet de Passages en Douane is required. This is a customs document which allows the holder to import his vehicle temporarily into a country without depositing large sums of money. The cost varies but is usually based on 200% of the vehicle's value. The fee paid is calculated as 10% of that value. This bureaucracy is just the beginning for anyone embarking on such a trip. Visas are necessary for most developing countries as well as for plenty of others, e.g. Australia. For some countries it is a complicated procedure, requiring photographs, letters of introduction as well as money.

FREIGHTING YOUR VEHICLE

If you have only limited holiday time, or your destination is across the world, you may decide to freight your vehicle by sea. Even to such localities as Iceland, freighting the vehicle and having passengers fly out will be cheaper and less time-consuming than the ferry crossing. A disadvantage could be that if it is your only vehicle you will have to do without it for the period of the sea crossings.

There are companies that advertise vehicle shipment but it is just as easy for you to contact a shipping agent (see your local Yellow Pages or try J.R. and C. Davies in Useful Addresses). The agent will find the best price and route for your needs (payment is invariably linked to the American dollar). Container shipment is expensive but is reasonably secure – you can be there when it is sealed and when it is opened. This does not guarantee safety, especially in certain African and South American ports. Amazing disappearing tricks from sealed containers are a common occurrence in the Kenyan port of Mombasa!

A cheaper alternative is shipment as deck cargo. At the end of shipment vehicles can look very sorry for themselves and any bare metal will stand out bright yellow-orange with rust. Some shipping groups suggest spraying the body and chassis with diesel to protect from the salt (Waxoil is perhaps a cleaner alternative) and you should certainly ensure that any equipment on roof racks is weatherproof.

Before shipment check that all locks work and keep a spare set of keys. Dock officials often lose vehicle keys. When arriving at the port to deposit or collect the vehicle have precise details of what is inside and even a plan of where the items are located. Have several photocopies available. Always be as helpful, pleasant and accommodating as possible to officials – the slightest sign that you are impatient will only cause problems. Allow several days for the collection of your vehicle from a port as filling in customs forms can

Fig. 9.10 Freighting may be a cheap alternative to ferries

be painstaking and slow. Details may have to be entered onto your passport.

Carry your vehicle registration documents and details of insurance at all times. Your normal insurance will not cover you for the shipment and so you must take out a separate maritime insurance policy. This will be arranged at your request by the shipping agent. Do not forget to include the value of equipment within your vehicle and if it includes food and other consumables the return journey can be insured for less. The general cost is about £10 per £1,000 for each boat trip. On top of freight cost and insurance will be a handling charge, not to mention a customs fee.

If you are involved in education in any way state this at the beginning of transactions with shipping agents as some cases are dealt with more leniently. Certain lines have special education rates and handling costs are sometimes waived.

Examples of shipping charges in 1993:

Grimsby-Reykjavik, return freight charge for LWB Land Rover, based on volume not weight: £500

Felixstowe-Mombasa, single freight charge for LWB Isuzu Trooper: £1,800. Expect to pay approximately £80 handling charge and £25 custom charges

Felixstowe-Dakar, single freight charge for 110 Land Rover: £800

Note: Freight is charged in US Dollars, and therefore costs will fluctuate with the exchange rate.

FIELD MAINTENANCE

A thorough service and maintenance check should be carried out before leaving home so that problems later on can be avoided. Know your limitations: perhaps it would be best to get a second opinion before setting out!

It is important to establish a maintenance routine when travelling: daily checks on tyres followed by a survey of nuts and bolts. Constant bumping over rough terrain stresses and loosens these. Often it is the older vehicle that gives fewest problems; they have already loosened up and then rusted to secure the bolt. A new vehicle suddenly put under stress is more likely to crack a windscreen or shed nuts. Running in the vehicle takes on a whole new meaning.

Faults developing on a vehicle need to be sorted out and not just left in the hope that they will go away – often they will get worse. But are you really capable of dropping the gearbox of a Land Rover to change the clutch thrust bearing? It may be better to trust your beloved steed to a 'bush' mechanic. He may not know the method depicted in the Solihull manual but the chances are he will make a good job of it. You may be put off the mechanic because he looks so young but most apprentices in Morocco, for example, start when they are 7 years old! Labour charges in Third World garages are usually very low in comparison to UK prices, but you will still have to haggle.

EXPEDITION PLANNING AND THE EAC

With hundreds of expeditions leaving the British shores each year, there has been a need for some coordinating body to disseminate information, so that help can be given to these and to forthcoming trips that are at present still scribbles on the back of an envelope. Unless carefully planned at the outset most ideas and dreams never become realised. That is why the Expedition Advisory Centre is so important.

The EAC provides information and training to those planning an overseas expedition. It was founded by the Royal Geographical Society and the Young Explorers' Trust, and has been sponsored by several companies over the years. The Centre is well established at the prestigious offices of the RGS in London and is an important first port of call. Thousands of expedition reports are on file, but several hours will be required to scan through even a dozen accounts. However, essential information can be gleaned to assist you to budget correctly as well as remove some of the possible pitfalls. It can be depressing as you see your dream trip disappearing beneath financial and bureaucratic problems. Alternatively, they can be amusing and can help you identify just the type of locality that you are after.

At the Centre there is a great aura of travel, in the form of the trappings of polar exploration, ancient maps of the Amazon and models of the Himalayas (and the best way to climb Everest). Try not to let it distract from the reality of your three-week jaunt to the French Pyrennees! No matter where you hope to travel abroad there will be something to help you. The EAC is mainly concerned with those planning scientific expeditions, mostly at undergraduate level, and, through its association with the Young Explorers' Trust, those leading school or youth expeditions, but it also gives valuable help to adventurous projects such as mountaineering, caving and canoeing, and it serves the independent and overland traveller.

Expedition reports are indexed by country, and any overlanders through Africa will find the Saharan country reports particularly good. These are all kept in the RGS map room, which is very convenient because as you read through the reports so the map you bought in W.H. Smiths becomes increasingly futile and the consultation of rarer, more detailed ones becomes essential. This can be especially valuable in helping you decide precisely which maps to buy and, as they are expensive, it can save a considerable amount of money. The EAC will also advise where the specialist maps can be obtained. All of this is open to the general public Monday to Friday, 10am-1pm and 2-5pm. There is also an extensive library, although this is only available to members of the RGS.

For those unable to reach London, the EAC provides notes for leaders visiting a specified country. These cost a nominal amount, and are compiled and up-dated for each enquiry for those seriously intending to plan an expedition. The more unusual the destination the longer they take to compile. The fact sheets include such things as general regulations pertaining to expeditions in that country, useful addresses and contacts within the UK and host country, and a reading list. Notes are attached on the availability of maps, abstracts of past expedition reports held at the RGS, and details of leaders that have recently planned expeditions to that country.

There are a number of very good publications produced by the EAC. The *Expedition Yearbook* is published at the end of each expedition year and includes details of all the important expeditions that left Britain during that time. Yearbooks get thicker each year with, on average, 400 trips listed. An important source of information for anyone contemplating their own venture would be *The Expedition Planner's Handbook & Directory*. With contributions by specialists from the world of science and exploration, it contains a wealth of knowledge to help you get organised, as well as facts on survival and the logistics of desert, polar and tropical forest expeditions, medical matters, photography, fund-raising and legal liability. Other publications from the EAC tend to be more specific such as Tom Sheppard's Desert Expedition book or *Expedition Navigation* by David Hall.

The EAC organise two training meetings every year, in May and November. These Independent Travellers Seminars are popular and inspiring. First-time travellers gain information and enthusiasm, whilst seasoned globetrotters gain the latest news and ideas. There are good speakers, plenty of people to swap ideas with, and displays and exhibits by leading equipment specialists. Everything from maps, charts, books, clothing, tents and flights across the globe can be bought!

Many would-be travellers know they have something to offer an expedition but do not feel capable of organising their own. For those with specialist skills to offer, particularly mechanics, there is a 'Register of Personnel available for Expeditions'. Those wishing to have their names and CVs added to this register should ask for the appropriate form. There is also a booklet (updated annually) entitled 'Joining an Expedition', which lists those organisations that regularly arrange expeditions abroad.

TRAVEL IN EUROPE

Planning and preparation

The Alps and Pyrennees are just a day's drive away from the English Channel. The opening of the channel tunnel will make the crossing to the Continent even easier, but it has already indirectly helped the traveller by stimulating the ferry companies to improve their sea crossings. Several ferry routes have now opened up to Northern Spain. It has never been simpler to tour the wild regions of Europe.

Where do you start the planning? Teletext is the most easily available method to obtain up-to-the minute information on road conditions, fuel prices, ferry routes and tourist exchange rates. There are even discounts on certain channel crossings. A visit to the nearest travel agent should provide you with all the ferry operators' brochures. Otherwise, phone the reservation departments direct. Motoring organisations are also good sources of information, particularly in assisting with motorway links through Europe. They should have the up-to-date toll rates for the French, Italian and Spanish autoroutes. The cost of these can soon mount up. In Switzerland a motorway permit is a legal requirement. This 'tax disc' can be purchased at the frontier or is obtainable in advance from the Swiss Tourist Office.

Most documents relate to the vehicle and driver. Take your driving licence, but an International Driving Permit, obtainable from motoring organisations, is needed in non-EEC countries. The Green Card, providing comprehensive insurance, is obtained from your insurance company. All countries to be visited have to be included on the document and it is best to name any that are in the vicinity of the intended destination. For example, when visiting Spain include Portugal and Andorra. More companies now provide one Green Card a year free of charge. The card may, sometimes, be purchased along with travel insurance. The latter is essential and it takes little time to organise as it is available from motoring organisations or through insurance brokers. Shop around, as costs for different time periods vary. Carry the vehicle registration document in case of an accident when proof of ownership may be required. Finally, when travelling in Spain you will need a Bail Bond ('get-out-of-jail-free card'). These are normally provided free with the green card or insurance package. They are important in the event of an accident to guarantee that the insurance company will pay up any damages.

Keep all of the documents together in an easily accessible but safe place. If you are stopped by the police they will be required. On-the-spot fines are now commonplace and the excuse of no money cuts no ice. Fines can be high, around £100. Road speeds and intricacies of motoring legislation vary between countries. For example, the carrying of spare light bulbs is compulsory in Spain, and not only is it obligatory to use a warning triangle in a breakdown but, if there are more than ten seats, as in a 110 County Land Rover, you officially need two. This information is often included with tourist office brochures or is found in good road atlases.

Dust and heat may cause engine hiccups when off roading in the day. Tyres are the biggest problem. Jagged rocks play havoc with side walls and replacements are expensive on the Continent. Dealerships of most vehicles are widely distributed so that obtaining spares should not be a problem. For the sake of a trouble-free trip, make sure that the vehicle is checked and serviced before leaving home. Inevitably, a holiday abroad will put more than the usual strain on the vehicle. Check the quality of the spare wheel; and it is always worth taking a small selection of vehicle spares or repair kits. It may be possible to persuade your friendly local stockist to give you a small kit on a sale-or-return basis. This would include bulbs, a collection of electrical items for a petrol engine (spark plug, condenser etc.) and maybe a selection of gaskets. Emergency repair compounds, such as those for exhaust, fuel tank and cooling system, are very useful along with epoxy resin glue. Waxing the bodywork before going away helps to reduce the effect of salt, sand and off-road scratching. For the latter, a wipe over with TCut upon returning home should restore the paintwork.

Obtaining food locally is not always possible, so consider taking a small quantity of dehydrated food. Drinking water is just as good if not better than the UK. Many taps with drinking water are specified with the label 'potable'. In very hot Mediterranean area, or if the source of drinking water is unclear, it is probably best to be safe by adding purification tablets to the water or buy mineral water.

Blue Gaz for cooking is available in all European countries, unlike Calor gas. The price of the Gaz varies enormously and not all bottle sizes are obtainable. This can be a problem when you try to exchange the empties. Rough camping is not always allowed in European countries and the cost of official sites varies considerably. The countries' tourist offices have all the relevant information on camping.

Some local currency for the intended countries should be obtained in the UK. Eurocheques are now widely accepted, particularly in the banks. Credit cards are great for fuel, as less cash has to be carried. Some garages in some countries do not accept cards, e.g. Germany.

CAMPING EQUIPMENT

Outlined below are a few suggestions to help if you intend to travel off the beaten track, i.e. with few amenities.

Camping may not be everyone's idea of fun but it is the only way to experience total independence with your 4x4. It can be as cheap or as expensive as you want to make it. Put another way, it can be as rough or as comfortable as you like. The essentials are:

- a sleeping bag
- somewhere to stay
- food and cooking

The first of these may not be high on everyone's priority list, but buying a sleeping bag needs careful consideration. It is worth spending a reasonable sum on a good bag. Looked after, it should give you long service. Cheap bags have little warmth and fail to roll up into a compact space – essential unless you are travelling in a 6x6 vehicle. Keeping warm has to be of paramount importance, and a good sleeping bag can sometimes allow you even to dispense with a tent.

Weather conditions are an all-important governing factor when considering which bag to buy. Remember that in hot climates it is surprising how cool it can become at night. Many good off-road places tend to be near mountain peaks. (For instance, camping out in the Sierra Nevada mountains of southern Spain in August is a chilling experience). The filling inside the bag is either of feather-down or a synthetic material such as Holofill. The former can give a very long life if well looked after, with the outer covering material usually disintegrating first. However, down can be expensive and when damp loses its effectiveness. The synthetic types depend on how the material is crimped to provide insulation. They are available in various ratings – the higher the number the warmer the filling. Synthetics continue to provide warmth, even when damp, and provide good ground insulation. Another useful point is that a small tear in the outer covering does not normally result in the filling falling out!

The shell covering material may be of a basic cotton or polyester. In the last decade, more bags have been made with materials such as Goretex. Basically, this is the same type of material used in non-stick saucepans (PTFE), and it acts as a thin membrane to waterproof the bag. However, the material also allows the body's moisture to pass through and prevent condensation inside the bag.

Over the years there has been a minimal change in the basic design of sleeping bags. Fashions may dictate variations in the covering, but if you do not require the most up-to-date colours a good bargain can be found, especially in autumn when most suppliers have extra discount available.

The most varied, and possibly expensive element in camping is accommodation. The four fundamental categories are:

- free-standing tent
- added sleeping accommodation to the vehicle, e.g. roof tent
- a factory-converted vehicle
- a trailer

The last can put constraints on where you can go.

A caravan, with its high sides and weight, is not a good proposition off road. Trailer tents are only marginally better. Some older, American trailers, e.g. Coleman, perform reasonably well on rocky mountain tracks as well as soft terrain. The chassis is strong, and has extra wide Armstrong radial tyres fitted for good flotation. Unless you consider an ex-NATO trailer with tyres of the same proportion as the vehicle, towing does limit the use of the vehicle.

An inexpensive ridge tent may be fine for a warm country, but going up-market to a thicker canvas will give a higher survival rate of the tent and camper. Repeated dismantling and reassembling will

Fig. 9.11 A Toyota VX Land Cruiser with a 4-berth roof tent and camping accessories. This is a typical hire arrangement in Australia. (Courtesy of Koala Campers, Australia)

Fig. 9.12 A demountable unit on the back of a pickup. Note side legs

effect a tent's life. Most tents have a sewn-in groundsheet, although this can soon become damaged by camping on rough ground. Placing another sheet of material down first will protect the groundsheet from being punctured. Take plenty of spare pegs. In mountainous and hot regions the pegs will soon be broken by the hard ground. Stuffiness within the canvas interior can be reduced by placing silver sheeting (e.g. survival blankets) on the roof of the tent. Some Continental manufacturers fit reflectant materials along the top of their tents.

Pod-type tents are the quickest to erect, with less pegging-out – very welcome at the end of a hard day. They have a series of hoops which keep the canvas up. Of all of these, the igloo variety usually provides the most room.

The roof tent is the quickest option, if rather expensive (starting price around £400). They tend to be more popular on the Continent, and certainly there is a wider selection in German or Italian camping stores. Brownchurch, Wilstow Ltd., and Afri-Quip Ltd. are three sources for roof tents in the UK. The beauty of the roof tent is the ease with which it is possible to stop anywhere and, with the release of a few catches, unfold it to produce accommodation with no pegging-out. A 4x4 can easily carry the large roof tents that are suitable for a family of four, unfolding either over the bonnet or out sideways to be supported by poles, which produces a shelter under which cooking is possible.

Going further up-market from the roof tents is the demountable accommodation. This is designed for pickups, typically found on Toyota Hilux and Land Rover Hicaps. They can have very plush interiors including beds, cooking facilities, fridge and even a toilet. The weight makes off roading a little restricting but the unit can be removed very simply. Legs are dropped down the side of the vehicle, and then the unit is jacked up clear of the vehicle. This can then be left on a campsite while you go off and explore.

EV Engineering produce internal demountable equipment. Although this is not as flexible as the external type it provides a good and temporary conversion for a long wheelbase Land Rover.

For several decades now, both Carawagon and Dormobile have made factory conversions of Land Rovers into campervans. Although basic, there are good, late, Series Two vehicles as well as Series Three available. New conversions of the Land Rover 110 can be obtained from the Wiltshire-based company, Overland, but are expensive.

One of the great aspects of independent travel is the chance to discover local cuisine or, alternatively, visit local markets and buy the fresh food and cook it yourself. The stove is therefore an essential piece of equipment that is useful, at any time, to brew up when out in the 4x4. Cost depends on the type of fuel used. The cheapest entry level stove is that produced by Gaz. Calor gas is easily obtainable in the UK but not abroad. The price of Blue Gaz refills varies between countries and not all sizes can be found. Stoves are produced by a wide number of manufacturers and come in various forms, from a single backpacker burner through to complex triple rings with grills. The main drawback is the low level of heat they produce. Meths and paraffin, used in such stoves as the famous Primus, can be pressurised to increase the heat output. The fuel can work out cheaper to buy but requires careful storage in between refilling the stove. Availability of these fuels is not widespread. The Trangia Meths stove has as an extra Gaz conversion kit, thus producing a dual purpose stove. Petrol stoves are more expensive but discharge more heat than the others and, as long as your vehicle runs on petrol, you only need to carry one fuel. Petrol is also the most widely available fuel. The Scandinavian company, Optimus, have for years produced very simple to use, compact, single burners. One model is a useful, multifuel burner. Slightly more complex, but with more variable models, are the American Coleman stoves. The small single-burner Coleman Peak stove can be easily carried on a plane and used with a hired 4x4 whilst in the bush. Run on unleaded petrol, they are very effective and easy to use. The two-burner and three-burner stoves fold up like a suitcase. If only leaded fuel is available the device that generates the petrol vapour tends to clog up with soot after a few hours. However, it can be cleaned, and spares, such as the generators, are all available and should be carried on a long trip. The pump requires an occasional squirt of WD40, particularly when used in hot, dusty climates. Sets of saucepans, with a kettle and stacking inside each other, are obtainable from most camping shops.

One of the greatest aspects of camping with a 4x4, particularly rough camping, is the opportunity you have of photographing the landscape. Usually, though, camping, off roading and photography do not mix. Condensation, mud and sand are incessant problems.

Fig. 9.13 Cooking stoves. At the back is a two-burner Coleman petrol stove. From left to right: Optimus (petrol), Coleman Peak (petrol) and Trangia (meths)

Protect the lens with a skylight filter and wrap the body of the camera in a polythene bag. Both protect against dust, and the filter is cheaper to replace than the lens when it falls out of the vehicle on to the ground.

EQUIPMENT CHECKLISTS

When you plan what needs to be taken on an expedition think of the essential life-and-death features first. Your vehicle could be your life-line so anything that will keep it going needs to be near the top of the list. Do not presume that food can just be picked up along the route. This might be all right in France or Germany but other European countries with true wildernesses, e.g. Iceland or even Spain, may not be so easy. In some remote villages the shops will only stock enough for the locals with just a little to spare. Always keep a supply of food: not just for a few days but for a week or more. Dehydrated foods take up little space or weight. Even if you intend to eat local foods most of the time your own supply can be a very important back-up. Having said that, different countries do have restrictions on food imports, so find out in advance from the relevant tourist board or embassy.

Tools

Workshop manual.
Feeler gauge.
A good pressure gauge: do not rely on those built into pumps.
Socket set with AF or metric, with extensions and T-bar.
Full combination set of spanners.
Extra ones of common sizes.
Thin-rimmed spanners.
Screwdrivers, assorted, incl. electrical and a short stubby flat-bladed one.
Heavy-duty wheelbrace.
Hand drill with drills 1/8 to 1/4 in.
Several cans of WD40 or equivalent.
Mixture of nuts and bolts and self-tapping screws.
Various lengths and gauges of wire.
Cold chisel.

Insulation tape.
Paint brush for cleaning purposes.
Small portable vice that can be clamped to the bumper.
Hacksaw and spare blades.
File (small and large).
Two short-handled shovels.
Hammer.
Various grades of emery wet and dry paper.
Brake pipe clamp.
Vernier caliper gauge.
Stilsons, 8-in.
Remote finger grip, 14-in.
Several size pliers.
Neon light circuit test driver.
Adjustable spanner.
Electric tyre pump, running from battery.

Vehicle spares

This list is compiled with particular reference to petrol-driven Land Rovers. Diesel engines require some similar spares and these are marked with a (D) against the part. In addition, for diesel, you will need to take spare fuel injectors and fuel filters. You local vehicle distributor, Unipart dealer or motor accessory shop will be able to modify this list to suit your particular vehicle. Many will supply these on a use or return basis. You may not be able to fit these items yourself but going to a garage with the spare part can save a tremendous amount of time.

Fuel pump repair kit (D).
Fuel pump (D).
Exhaust valve (D).
Decoke set (D).
Spark plugs.
Distributor cap.
Coil.
Contact set.
Condenser.
Rotor arm.
New or reconditioned water pump (D).
Carburettor repair kit (D).
Fuel injectors for diesel engine (D).
Brake hoses for front and rear (D).
Oil seal kits, front and rear axle (D).
Clutch master cylinder kit (D).
Slave cylinder kit (D).
Bushes and shackle pin (D).
Universal joint (D).
Brake master cylinder kit (D).
Brake wheel cylinder kit or disc caliper seal kit (D).
Rear half-shaft (D).
Drive flange (D).
Radiator cap (D).
Set of light bulbs (D).
Fan belt (D).
Set of radiator hoses and heater hoses (D).
Hose clips. (D)
Clutch plate and cover (D).
Clutch thrust release bearing (D).

Spare leaf springs: it will probably suffice to take just the first and second leaves, which can be fitted on to the bumper for carriage. For this use the spare spring shackles and pins (D).
Two litres of brake/clutch fluid (D).
Five litres of gear oil EP90 (D).
Exhaust bandages and silencer repair paste (D).
Instant gasket (D).
Three metres of flexible fuel pipe (D).
Shock absorber bushes (D).
Radseal (D).
Petrol Patches (D).
Hose bandage (D).
Epoxy resin (D).
WD40 or equivalent (D).
Engine oil. Calculate the amount and then double it. Land Rovers tend to be thirsty for oil, especially if the terrain is hard going.
1 or 2 inner tubes for tyres.
Puncture repair kit, rubber mallet, tyre levers.
Swarfega.
Spare set of ignition keys.
Fire extinguisher suitable for petrol and electrics.
Sheet to cover vinyl seats in hot climate.

This is a list of the items that we would carry on a four to five week trip.

You will find that many guide books include a list four times its length. Other things could go wrong but these items have always covered the problems that we have encountered and you have to strike a balance in what to take. They will also pack down into one large box (clutch plate excepted). Ex-ammunition boxes, obtainable from many army surplus stores, can be bolted to the roof rack for storing the spares and then padlocked.

The greater the availability of spares at your destination the fewer items you will have to take; so contact your vehicle manufacturer for a list of distributors and spares outlets in the country you intend to visit. Land Rover produce a book with all this information. In the past we have occasionally taken the manufacturer's spares catalogue (rather bulky and heavy) so that the correct spare could be identified. Normally this can be dispensed with.

Expansion of fluids in the heat can cause leakages and even bursting of bottles. So that other equipment is not contaminated, pack bottles of fluids in tough polythene bags. If you are driving a diesel vehicle in wet, hot or dusty conditions carry extra fuel filter elements. Also consider taking an oil filter for an engine oil change whilst away. For a long overland trek it can be advisable to fit two fuel filters instead of just the usual one, as a back-up filter could make the difference between running or breakdown. Outside Europe there is more chance of diesel being contaminated. Instead of obtaining fuel from the usual type of pump it may be from a fuel dump contained in 45-gallon drums. In these situations begin with a sniff test. If the diesel is contaminated with petrol, even as little as 2 per cent, it becomes more volatile and damages the head and pistons. Water cannot easily be identified by smell but if it does get past the fuel filters it will damage the distributor pump and injectors in a very short time.

Camping equipment

This is only intended to be a rough guide and will of course need to be pruned and added to according to your requirements.

Passport.
Vehicle log book.
Green card.
International driving licence.
Insurance policy.
Boat tickets.
Letter of introduction.
Tents.
Spare pegs, mallet, spare guys.
Repair kit for tent.
Dining shelter, poles and ropes.

Cooking stove, including spares,
Funnel for petrol and fuel as
  necessary.
Cooking pans, pressure cookers,
  kettle.
Bowls and washing-up liquid.
Scourers, J-cloth.
Tea towels.
Cooking utensils including small
  whisk.
Can openers.

Matches (including some water-proof and windproof ones).
Folding chairs.
Separate water carriers.
Measuring jug.
Unbreakable mugs, plates, cutlery.
Bin liners for rubbish.
Spare polythene bags.
Light, torch.
Camp table.
First-aid kit.
Dustpan and brush.
Tarpaulins and rope.
Bungie luggage straps.
Maps and books.
Penknife.
Toilet tent, toilet and sanitary fluid.

Spray disinfectant.
Insect repellent; try several brands, e.g. Jungle Formula, Midge-spray.
Air bed and pump (electric pumps that run off the battery are available).
Bucket (collapsible ones available from camp shops).
Water purification tablets or sodium dichioroisocynanurate dihydrate.
Shower or garden spray.
Labels, string, Sellotape, paper, notebook, pencil, pen.
Compass, whistle.
Camera equipment, film, binoculars.

Medical supplies

The following list offers suggestions for the treatment of ailments most commonly encountered. In any case contact your GP before you leave as some useful drugs are only available on prescription.

Congestion, catarrh and rhinitis – long-acting decongestant, e.g. *Dimotapp.*
Painful and sore throat – antiseptic painkilling oral rinse, throat lozenges.

Diarrhoea and sickness – *Immodium* for diarrhoea, *Lomotil* for both. The latter is suitable for children. Persistent diarrhoea causes loss of salts. *Rehydrate* helps to restore the balance, as do *Electrosol* tablets. Vomiting – anti-emetic, e.g. *Stemitil*
Indigestion – antacids.
Colic – antispasmodics, e.g. *Buscopan* (suitable for children).
Travel sickness – e.g. *Stugeron.*

Dressings – crepe bandages, antiseptic swabs, plasters, butterfly sutures, non-allergenic plaster, e.g. *Micropore.*

Headache and general pain – painkiller, e.g. *Paracetamol.*
Hay fever and other allergies – anti-histamine tablets.
Chafing and sore skin – an anti-fungal cream with hydrocortisone and an anti-inflammatory, e.g. *Econacort.*

Insect bites – anti-histamine, e.g. *Anthisan* cream.
Muscular pain – e.g. *Algesal* cream.
Eye infection – e.g. *Murine* eye drops.
A course of general antibiotics for possible bacterial infection, including a tooth abcess.

Check which, if any, innoculations are necessary for the countries to be visited. Tetanus should always be kept up to date. Typhoid is now becoming available in tablet form. The vaccine for Hepatitis is a single dose of gamma-globulins, injected just before departure as this only lasts for six months. For regular travellers the Havrex innoculation is better. It involves a booster two weeks after the first, but lasts for ten years. Polio boosters should be taken before any trip to Africa or South America.

10

Where to Go

Most countries have their green lanes but some more than others and the chances are they will not be green! Define your limits clearly from the start. How much time and money do you want to spend? Do you want a holiday fortnight or a year-long expedition? Given below are just a few suggested areas for travel. Those in Europe and North Africa can be reached fairly easily from the United Kingdom and have good potential for off roading. Circumstances change from year to year and in all cases you should obtain and study a good map prior to your departure. There is nothing better than thorough preparation, and, please, maintain the green lane code wherever you travel.

EUROPE

IRELAND

An amazing place and the green lanes are actually signposted! The west coast from County Donegal in the north to County Kerry in the south is breathtaking, with some of the most beautiful scenery possible. The laid-back attitude of the people is catching. Rarely will you pay for parking near the beach, and usually you can drive on to and along the sand, camping in the dunes.

There are numerous green lanes but check the map – they tend to be left to become overgrown. If you meet farmers, the chances are

---

Illustration, facing page:
Fig. 10.1 Off road high in the Ecrins National Park, French Alps

they will be very friendly and want you to stop for a chat. Most routes are remote and even on the main roads traffic is almost non-existent.

The limestone region called the Burren is on the coast of County Clare. It is well worth a visit and is a good place in which to become accustomed to Ireland's pace of life.

FRANCE

Being the largest country in Europe but with a population density similar to the United Kingdom it is not surprising that France has some remote and beautiful sites. but care must be exercised off road as there is a strong lobby against the activity. Check with detailed maps, such as the 'Institut Geographique National' Green Map Series (1:100,000) and the Blue (1:500,000) Series, that the tracks are for the public. The Pyrenees is an especially good region as there are so many tracks and trails to follow. There are even commercial enterprises that will take you for off-road holidays, with or without your own 4x4. The Alps have stunning scenery but the steepness of the terrain makes long distance tracks somewhat elusive. Centrally located in the French Alps, the Ecrins and Queyras National Parks have to be amongst the most amazing places in Europe. The latter park has fewer visitors and more tracks. Other areas which are noteworthy include the Auvergne in the Massif Central, the Ardèche on the way to Provence, the Jura Mountains near Switzerland and the Ardennes just to the north. In all cases, this is a holiday destination where the traveller is never far from civilisation and a café bar for a cool drink.

SPAIN AND PORTUGAL

Forget Torremolinos or the Costa Brava, explore Spain's wild and majestic interior. Much of the country is above the height of Snowdon and regularly rises to above 2,000 m. High sierras (mountain ranges) are liberally scattered across the country and each is distinct, with its own typical flora and fauna.

In the north the mountains begin near the Mediterranean Sea and stretch like a backbone for over 1,000 km across the country, reaching the Atlantic coast above Portugal. To the east they are the Spanish Pyrenees whilst to the west they become the Cantabrican Mountains. Numerous areas can be explored off-road.

Fig. 10.2 Clearing boulders from a track in the Aigues Tortes National Park, Spanish Pyrenees

The Firestone maps are particularly detailed with red dotted lines – temptingly called 'Jeep Tracks' – crossing some of the large, desolate areas. Many of these tracks supply very remote villages high up in the ranges but in a new policy of road building, tracks are slowly being paved. This is happening in those areas now opening up for tourism such as the Picos de Europa. So be quick or they could be gone. Many of the National Parks, e.g. the Aigues Tortes in the Pyrenees, have some spectacular routes only passable with 4x4s. They are very rocky and steep with occasional streams and rivers. You are likely to meet Santana Land Rover taxis which take tourists from nearby villages up into the mountains.

Some sierras have very restricted access, like the Guadarrama mountains north of Madrid. Heed the small signs that are fixed to trees indicating private land. The Sierra Nevada mountains of the south are truly magnificent. One can take the paved road from Granada, the highest road in Spain (and, reputedly, in Europe). Alternatively, there are a number of excellent dirt tracks coming from the south crossing a beautiful region called the Alpujarras. One can easily get lost on the many routes so have a good map. The main track to ascend Pico de Valeta (approximately 3,400 m) begins near Capileira. It is a long, hot climb. Also in the south, near Almeria, is the Badlands. This semi-desert region had dried up river beds with the occasional mini-oasis and was home to the filming of the spaghetti-westerns of the 1960s.

If you like Spain then you will really like Portugal – fewer cars, delightful people and roads that just merge into tracks. Camping and living costs are much cheaper than Spain.

EASTERN BLOC

With the opeing up of the previously Communist eastern bloc countries there has been a steady increase in tourism to countries such as Czech, Hungary and what was East Germany. These are a delight to visit, but do bear in mind the culture difference that still exists. Many of the roads are of very poor standard. Country roads are unsignposted and are often just graded tracks where a twenty-year-old Trabant is the normal car to see. In these countries the 4x4 is a useful vehicle with which to negotiate the pot-holes of the public highways and has the strength to survive the rigours of touring the country. Pilfering is prolific. In cities like Prague watch out for your windscreen wipers!

SCANDINAVIA

Norway is a very long and narrow country with several large icecaps. The scenery is spectacular but considerable tarmac driving is required to reach the various regions where off roading is possible. Within the Arctic Circle and around the icecaps there is considerable off-road potential. Fuel prices are among the most expensive in Europe. Sweden has marginally cheaper living costs. The arctic tundra area of Lapland is particularly exciting. There are no border restrictions between the countries and it is easy to move back and forth. Part of the preparation for the trip should include a way of dealing with the prolific numbers of mosquitoes and horseflies.

By comparison, Iceland has what other areas of Scandinavia has to offer (except the vast forests) and no biting flies. Besides which

Fig. 10.3 The ultimate off-road experience – crossing Iceland's interior wilderness

it has volcanoes and hot springs, more glaciers and a vast, remote interior.

Although an expensive place to reach and live, Iceland remains one of the ultimate off-bitumen experiences. Even the main road around the country is not completely sealed. It has every aspect of scenery you could want, from mountains, fjords, glaciers and volcanoes to cold deserts of outwash sand, waterfalls and rivers. Crossing the interior takes several days and can involve blizzards in the middle of summer. It is potentially dangerous and must not be undertaken lightly. Routes are marked with yellow stakes at 100 m intervals and drivers must remain on these where possible. There is concern that serious damage to the environment will occur if irresponsible drivers disregard this basic code. Numerous routes branch out across the country, and so a wide choice of tracks can be undertaken, some of which can be very demanding.

Iceland is deceptively large with very few people and you really do need your 4x4 to see it. There is nowhere quite like it.

ASIA

The early Land Rover overland expeditions to Australia of the 1950s had the best of travel when there were few political problems when driving to India and Singapore. The Foreign Office now discourages such travel because of problems in Afghanistan, Iran and Iraq. To compensate however, it is now possible to go deeper into what were the soviet republics. During September 1992 the first Paris-Moscow-Beijing rally-raid took place, taking in most of the route through the Asian mountains and deserts.

TURKEY

Of all the countries of Asia, Turkey is one of the most accessible for those travelling from the UK. Travelling through Europe it is possible to drive overland through Hungary, Bulgaria and Greece. Turkey has a wide range of contrasting landscapes and in the last decade has become 'discovered'. However, most tourists remain on the western Mediterranean coast. The interior is fascinating with mountain ranges and a complete treasure trove of archaeological

Fig. 10.4 Range Rover towing a Coleman trailer/camper off road in Turkey

sites and artefacts. Dirt tracks dissect the stunning countryside. The only way of seeing the real Turkey is in a 4x4 off the bitumen. The area to the south of the capital, Ankara, is particularly wild and with few roads. The desert-like upland steppe country has ancient tumuli that look like pyramids. Further east is a wilderness, known by the ancients as Commagene, set around the River Euphrates. At the heart of this spectacular place is Adiyaman, a city few tourists have the chance to visit. To the north, mountains rise to over 2,500m and a FWD vehicle is the only way of exploring the terrain.

A Suzuki can be hired in Ankara but no vehicle rental is cheap. One of the best compromises during the summer months is a more reasonable Peugeot 305 which can cope with much of the terrain.

At the present time it is best to avoid the south eastern region where it borders on Iran and Iraq.

AFRICA

Unfortunately the Dark Continent is no longer the safe expeditionaries' dream. Political strife and famine have made the crossing of the Sahara a nightmare. At the time of writing, the route through to Tamanrasset is impassable due to the closure of Morocco's southern border with Algeria. Mali is also busy with guerrilla warfare. Vehicles that do make it as far as Tam are often hijacked and used to further the war effort. The alternative to crossing the north is to freight the vehicle down to Dakar in Senegal. From here it is possible to cross West Africa to Cameroon. This is then a suitable starting point for East Africa, although obtaining the necessary travel documents could prove difficult. To the south is the Angolan problem, and political issues in central Africa still make any travel there hazardous. Perhaps the greatest problem is the speed of change. The visas you obtain in the UK for African countries could be invalid by the time you arrive in the continent. Many travellers now allow plenty of time and decide on routes by using local information as they go; visas can be obtained along the way but remember to take a good supply of passport-size photographs and letters of introduction.

Several books deal with specific routes across the region (see Swain & Snyder) and these give fairly detailed notes on the countries.

Fig. 10.5 Passing through a remote village in the High Atlas mountains of Morocco. A culture shock in the extreme

NORTH AFRICA

A hard three-day drive from England will get you to the south coast of Spain, even in a relatively slow Land Rover. By boat from Algeciras, near Gibraltar, it is a mere 90-minute crossing to Morocco. Tunisia can be reached by a 24-hour ferry crossing from Genoa. Living in North Africa is cheap and off roading can start almost immediately. Morocco has the most varied scenery with several very extensive mountain ranges. The Middle Atlas has some of the last forests of cedar, whilst the High Atlas (reaching almost 5,000m) is rocky scrubland. All have amazing cross-country routes through gorges and remote mountain villages. The Sahara Desert is not all 'Beau Geste' sand dunes but is mainly of stones and rock. Erg Chebbi at the end of the Tafilalt oases road is the only large expanse of dunes in Morocco. Although it is not possible to go much farther south because of the Algerian border there are several off-road routes westwards to Zagora.

WEST AFRICA

Freighting an expedition vehicle to Dakar is the best way to see West Africa. It has the richest cultural mixture of any part of the continent and yet in the past was often disregarded by overlanders. Travel is relatively straightforward between the countries, but because the economy is linked with the French franc it is not the cheapest of African regions. Allow plenty of time to obtain visas and fill up with fuel whenever possible.

There is a wide range of diseases almost unique to West Africa, so take suitable precautions; research this well in advance. Guinea, on the southern border with Senegal, has particularly beautiful country. Road quality is poor throughout but the people are very friendly.

CENTRAL AFRICA

The heart of Africa, this is the most difficult area to cross although the sight of rainforest and mountains makes it worthwhile. Driving conditions can be particularly difficult and treacherous. Several expeditions we know of ended abruptly in Cameroon and Zaire when the vehicles became completely stuck in deep glutinous mud, which is typical of highways in the wet season. Within Zaire the roads are so heavily rutted by large trucks that ground clearance beyond that of a Land Rover may be required. Expect to become caught up in jams of two-wheel drive lorries stuck in the mud, sometimes there for weeks!

EAST AFRICA

Although many overland expeditions hope to end up here there are plenty of 4x4 rentals possible in countries like Kenya. Alternatively, join up with one of the organised safaris which take tourists into the game parks. Uganda is not geared up for the enthusiast requiring a hired 4x4. They have precious little fuel, most of which is obtained on the black market, let alone having vehicles for hire.

SOUTHERN AFRICA

This is generally well organised with good roads to traverse the countries. FWD is only necessary if you wish to go deep into the game reserves, and then a commercial package is probably advisable.

AMERICA

South America is not such a no-go area as Africa, but to freight or hire a 4x4 there is much more expensive. Travel between countries is relatively straightforward but, again, political instability makes an expedition a hazardous affair with a minimum of backup. Land Rovers are well known in Africa but are comparatively rare here. Old Land Cruisers or American Eagle/Wrangler Jeeps are more the norm. The best option is to select individual countries, such as Venezuela or Ecuador, and operate just within that one place. The latter country has all the big car rental firms so that a Ford 4x4 Escaper could be used to explore parts of the Amazon basin or the superb off-road tracks of the Cotopaxi National Park. Fuel is very cheap and traffic very limited.

Some travellers attempt the ill-fated Pan American Highway. At best it is a tarmac road but in most places is little more than an overgrown track. Some sections have disappeared completely. This may be the only way to reach Chile which, despite its political problems, has some very impressive off-road tracks for those venturing into the Andes.

North America is a different story with a well established off-road scene. Most long tracks are documented and well used. Some appear regularly in the off-road calendar, such as the annual Jeep Jamboree in the Sierra Nevada. Local tourist offices usually have information and maps.

AUSTRALIA

Australia is the last great wilderness that can be explored with controlled safety. Each year flights to Cairns or Perth become cheaper and within reach of the average family. All trips require careful planning and preparation. Remember that most of these regions were the death of early explorers only a century ago. Almost every type of terrain can be found in Australia, including vast sandy deserts, extensive rainforest and high snowy, mountain ranges. A year would not be long enough to spend in the country if you wanted to sample all the delights on offer.

There is a choice of either hiring a 4x4, buying one or freighting. The last option is not really viable from the UK. For a long term trip, buy a vehicle locally. There tends to be a glut of secondhand 4x4s in Cairns and so the prices are good. It is possible to obtain a vehicle which has already been kitted out for an expedition. Another good reason for buying locally is that the engines on vehicles such as Land Rovers are different from the UK and spares will be easy to obtain. Hiring is the only option for a short term trip. Companies like Territory Rent-a-car and Koala Rentals have a wide range of 4x4s, including Suzukis, Mitsubishis and Toyotas. The Toyotas come in anything from a three-door model up to the top spec VX Land Cruiser with accompanying roof tent for four persons. It is even possible to hire ten- or twelve-seater Toyota Troopers, based on the 70 Series. All can be obtained with full camping equipment supplied. The hire companies will also give advice on suitable treks. The country is very geared up for FWD and the great outdoors. If you do not want to go it alone it is possible to join up with one of the many off-road companies,, which lead expeditions and have full backup. However, you can still drive your own (or hired) 4x4. The final alternative is to book a passage on a commercial outback expedition. The tourist boards from the various states are full of adverts for this type of trip.

Cairns is a common place to begin a FWD trek. The sealed road stops just north of the town and the dirt roads begin. During the wet season it is a major expedition to reach Cape York on the northern tip of Queensland. Creek crossings through the rainforest make this a trip to remember. The Kimberley district of northwest Australia is an area the size of the UK with only the occasional track to follow. Much of the terrain is scrub forest on tablelands. The Gibb River starts here and it is possible to follow the river to the sea. The coastline of Kimberley, hundreds of miles long, is completely devoid of any settlement, and the traveller must be completely self sufficient. This also applies in the Bungle Bungles, next to Kimberley: an off-roader's dream come true. To the south of Kimberley is the Great Western Desert. A sealed road now cuts Australia in two as it passes from Darwin in the north, through Alice Springs, to Adelaide in the south. From Alice Springs it is possible to radiate out into the Macdonnell Ranges. This highland region in the centre of Australia has great rocky chasms and gorges with remote oases to explore. Sand and bull-dust makes a 4x4 vehicle essential. As well as having some of the best off-road terrain there are a number of classic green lanes. Some stretch for over 600 miles. These long cross-country tracks have names like the Gibb River Road, which is an old drovers' track through the Kimberley. The 350-mile Birdsville Track runs from the town of that name in Queensland to Marree in South Australia and is quite feasible with any 4x4. On the other hand the Canning Stock Route, which crosses the Great Sandy and Gibson Deserts, requires considerable planning and careful navigation. The Gunbarrel Highway links Ayers Rock with Laverton in Western Australia. Rocky and with sections of soft sandy conditions, it passes through Aboriginal land. Generally, permission and a permit are required before crossing such land. Permission is by no means automatic, and in some areas, such as Arnhem Land to the east of Darwin, it is never granted.

Before any exploration of the outback is made, it is necessary to contact the local police. Usually, they have a noticeboard with the latest information on the tracks. During the wet season conditions change rapidly.

POLITICS & CULTURE

The essence of travel is the quest for something new, something different. To this end, expeditions set out on a shoestring to go where no one has gone before. Unfortunately, many are ill-prepared not just financially and logistically but for the culture shock of a developing country. There is a fine line between involvement and detachment: between living with the locals or viewing them through a Land Rover windscreen as if driving through an amusement park. Travellers should always remember that they are ambassadors for their country and treat the people with respect even when under duress. An African border crossing with a bureaucratic guard exercising his limited power can be the ultimate trying condition. Remember, you are just experiencing the local culture.

The political map of the world changes rapidly. At the time of writing conditions are slowly improving in Mali but possibly deteriorating in Niger. Algeria is still no-go. The British consulates in the countries one visits can be very helpful but must never be expected to bail you out of a situation that careful planning would have avoided. If an area to be crossed appears to be dubious, contact the Foreign Office for the latest information. The current travel desk number is 071 270 4129.

Glossary

ABS anti-lock braking system.
Airlockers air operated diff. locks.
Approach angle the angle of a slope which a vehicle can approach and climb without the front touching the ground.
Axle articulation movement of opposing wheels on the same vehicle.
bhp brake horsepower.
Bridle a short connecting strap to convert a single line pull to two points.
Departure angle the angle of a slope a vehicle can depart from without touching the ground.
Differential device for transmitting power to two points but allowing one point to go faster than the other.
Differential (diff.) lock a lock to make the differential transmit equal power to two points. Central diff. lock: a third differential, located in transmission to stop wind up.
Dog clutch simple form of connecting drive to other devices, e.g.the winch.
Double rigged a system of ropes or cables round a pulley to obtain mechanical advantage.
Engine braking using the compression of the engine through the gearbox to retard motion.
Floating axle (fully) where the drive shaft is completely independent of the hub bearings.
Floating axle (semi) where the drive shaft supports the hub bearings.
Four-wheel drive (FWD) all wheels are driven.
Free wheeling hub (FWH) device which enables the front wheels to be disengaged from the front drive train.
Ground anchor stake or device for fixing rope or cable to ground.
Ground clearance measurement between the lowest point of vehicle and ground.
High-lift jack jack capable of lifting heavy loads very high.
Kinetic Energy Recovery Rope (KERR) rope used in technique utilising the force stored in this special, stretchy rope for recovery.
Live axle supports the weight of the vehicle and contains the drive to the wheels.
LWB long wheel base.
OHC over-head camshaft.
Ramp breakover angle a three-point angle measured where front and rear wheels contact the ground and the lowest mid point of the vehicle.
Shackle attachment device in the shape of a U with a pin through both ends making a D shape.
Snatch rope alternative name for rope used in KERR technique (see above).
Strop a strap with a loop each end used for connecting rope/cable, e.g. to an anchor.

Suspension travel the distance a wheel will travel between its highest and lowest point.

SWB short wheelbase.

Torque the twisting force of the engine.

Transfer box secondary gear box that splits drive to rear and front of vehicle.

Transmission transmits drive from engine to wheels.

Transmission brake an independent handbrake which works on the transmission.

Transmission wind-up components of transmission getting very tight because wheels rotating at different speeds.

Tyreseal the seal of the tyre to the wheel rim.

V8 an engine of eight cylinders arranged in a V configuration.

Wheelbase the measurement between front and rear axles.

Useful Addresses

Books On 4x4s and off roading:
LRO Bookshop, Netherfield House, Chedgrave, Norwich NR14 6NQ
  Tel: (0508) 28068
Camper Conversions
E.V. Engineering Ltd., Expedition Vehicles, Aysgarth Road, Waterlooville
  Tel: (0705) 241215
Club addresses
The All-Wheel Drive Club, P.O. Box 6, Fleet, Hants GU13 9YY
The Association of Rover Clubs, 10 Highfield Road, Bagslate, Rochdale
  OL11 5RZ
The Austin Gypsy Register, 8 Thoresby Court, Stem Lane, New Milton,
  Hants BH25 5UJ
The Jeep Register, 252 Lon Inwydd, Trehafren, Newton, Powys
Lada Niva Owner's Club, 12 Paddock Close, Clapham, Bedford
Land Rover Series 1 Club, East Foldhay, Zeal Monachorum, Crediton,
  Devon EX17 6DH
Land Rover Series 2 Club, PO Box 1609, Yatton, Bristol BS19 4QP
The Military Vehicle Trust, 6 Brackenbury, The Drove, Andover, Hants
  SP10 3PU
The Mitsubishi Motor Owner's Club, Colt Car Co., Watermoor,
  Cirencester, Glos. GL7 1LF
National 39-45 Military Vehicle Group, 18 Preston Close,
  Stanton-under-Bardon, Leics
North Devon Off Road Club, 99 Chanters Road, Bideford, Devon, EX39
  2QP
Range Rover Register, Cwm Cockern, Bettws, Newtown, Powys SY16 3LQ
The Rhino Club, Suzuki (GB) Ltd, 46-62 Gatwick Road, Crawley, West
  Sussex RH10 2XF
Toyota Owner's Club, The Quadrangle, Station Road, Redhill, Surrey RH1
  1PX
Dehydrated foods
Brooke Bond Foods Ltd, Leon House, High Street, Croydon CR9 1JQ
  (discount service for expeditions buying in bulk)
McDougalls Catering Foods Ltd, Worcester House, Basingstoke Road,
  Reading RG2 0QW
Engine Conversions/modifications
Many of these have agents.
Steve Parker, Heally Dell, Rochdale, OL12 6BG (0706) 350 140
Turbo Technics Ltd., Brackmills, Northampton (0604) 764005
SMC Industrial, Unit 1, Aifield Way, Somerford, Christchurch, Dorset
  (0202) 480414 (Nissan Diesel Engines, 3.1 TDi Isuzu engines, automatic
  gearboxes)
BMW Diesel Engines, American Engines. (0722) 414111

Mazda Engines, MD Engineering, Station Works, Old North Road, Bourn, Cambridge. (0954) 719549/719633

Isuzu TDi, M Burgins of Powys

Turbocharger Conversions, DMS, Unit 1 Milne House, Speedwell Mill, Millers Green, Wirksworth, Derby. (0629) 824969

Warwick 4x4 Ltd., Budbrooke Industrial Estate, Warwick CV34 5XH. Tel: 0926 410090 (also body/suspension conversions)

Expeditions For camping and clothing equipment:

Field and Trek (Equipment) Ltd, 3 Wates Way, Brentwood, Essex CM15 9TB Tel: (0277) 233122

Wilderness Ways, 26-28 Park Road, Chesterfield, Derbyshire S40 1XZ, Tel: (0246) 201437

Touring Sport - Rosker Ltd, Unit 13, Quay Lane, Gosport, Hants PO12 4LT Tel: (0705) 528711

Global Positioning Systems/Satellite Navigation

ElectroTech, Head Office, Unit 6, Drury Way Ind. Estate, Laxcon Close, London NW10 0TG. Tel: 081 451 6766

Insurance If you have difficulty insuring camping equipment, contact:

Fennell Turner and Taylor Ltd, Southway House, South Way, Cirencester, Glos. GL7 1HL

Land Rovers (ex-military) For jerrycans, trailers, spares etc., try:

Brooklyn Engineering (Southern) Ltd, Hursley Road, Chandler's Ford, Eastleigh, Hants SO5 1JH Tel:(0703) 252281

Crook Brothers, Station Road Depot, Hoghton, Preston Tel: (025 485) 2457

Keith Gott, 58 Battersea Bridge Road, London SW11 3AG Tel: 071 228 2850

P.R.B. Services, 275 Tong Road, Leeds 12 Tel: (0532) 796039 (Specialist in 101 forward control Land Rovers.)

P.A. Blanchard & Co, Clay Lane, Shiptonthorpe, York YO4 3RU

'Lumenition'

Lumenition Ltd, 640 Ripple Road, Barking, Essex IG11 0RU

Maps W.H.Smith's and the Ordnance Survey can supply most maps of the British Isles.

For worldwide maps the most comprehensive range is from Stanford's, who will send maps mail order.

Stanford's Map Centre, 12-14 Long Acre, Covent Garden, London WC1

Dick Phillips, Whitehall House, Nenthead, Alston, Cumbria LA22 0HP (Specialist in maps of Iceland.)

New Accessories/parts suppliers For most off-road accessories including ARB products, winches, recovery equipment, land anchors, etc. try:

David Bowyer's Off Road Centre, East Foldhay, Zeal Monachorum, Credition, Devon EX17 6DH. Tel: (0363) 82666

Merlin Motorsport, Castle Combe Circuit, Chippenham, Wilts SN14 7EX. Tel: (0249) 782101

Trans-Atlantic 4x4 UK Ltd., Unit C, Venture Cres. Motorway Link Ind. Estate, Alfreton, Derby DE5 7RA. Tel: (0773) 540910

Janspeed Engineering Ltd., Castle Road, Salisbury, Wilts SP1 3SQ. Tel: (0722) 321833 (performance)

North Staffs 4x4 Centre, Lightwood Road, Longton, Stoke-on-Trent, Staffs. Tel: (0782) 593091

Inta Town Tyres, Hallgate, Pocklington, York. Tel: (0759) 305273 (tyres & wheels)

AEW Paddock Motors Ltd., The Cliff, Matlock, Derbyshire DE4 5EW. Tel: (0629) 584498

John Craddock (Land Rover), 70-76 North Street, Bridgtown, Cannock, Staffs WS11 3AZ Tel: (0543) 577207

Birmingham Land Rover Services Ltd., 480 College Road, Erdington, Birmingham B44 0HL Tel: (021) 373 7425

R.K. Automotive, Unit 5, Tamworth Enterprise Park, Mariner, Lichfield Road Industrial Estate, Tamworth, Staffs. Tel: (0827) 63 866

Famous Four, Tatershall Way, Fairfield Ind. Estate, Louth, Lincs. Tel: (0507) 609444

Acoustikit Soundproofing, Leesbrook, Lees Road, Lees, Oldham OL4 5JL Tel: (061) 652 2773

Dixon-Bate, Unit 45, First Ave, Deeside, Clwyd CH5 2LG Tel: (0244) 288925

Kenlowe Ltd., Maidenhead, Berks SL6 6QU Tel: (0628) 823303

Rimmer Bros., Triumph House, Sleaford Road, Bracebridge Heath, Lincoln LN4 2NA Tel: (0522) 568000 (stainless-steel exhaust systems)

Shurflo Euro Division Ltd., Liberty House, 105 Bell Street, Reigate, Surrey RH2 7JB Tel: (0737) 242290

Bearmach PLC, Maindy Road, Cardiff CF2 4XN Tel: (0222) 341313 (Specialist equipment)

ERG Plastics, Tel: (0923) 211052

Off-road schools in the UK The following are member companies of The Off-Road Training Association (TORTA):

David Bowyer's Off Road Centre, East Foldhay, Zeal Monachorum, Crediton, Devon EX17 6DH Tel: David Bowyer (0363) 82666

Highland Drovers, Croft of Kincardine, Boat of Garten, Inverness-shire PH24 3BY Tel: Graham Clarke (047 983) 329

Landcraft Off Road, 'The Steppes', Pen-Y-Ball Hill, Holywell, Clwyd CH8 8SZ Tel: David Mitchell (0352) 711855

Ronnie Dale Off-Road Adventure Driving School, Whiteburn, Abbey St Bathams, Duns, Berwickshire TD11 3RU Tel: Ronnie Dale (03614) 244

Rough Terrain Training Ltd, Old Gibraltar Quarry, Temple Mill, Sibford Gower, Oxfordshire OX15 5BZ Tel: Peter Clifford (029578) 8414

Others include

Warwickshire College Off-Road Driving School, Moreton, Morrell, Warwick, Warwickshire CB35 9BL

Lakeland 4x4 Driving Experience, Lakeland Village, Newby Bridge, Ulverston, Cumbria LA12 8PX

Wessex 4x4 Driving Experience, Combe Grove Manor, Brassknocker Hill, Monkton Combe, Bath BA2 7HS

Roof racks Also water filters and other specialist expedition equipment:
Brownchurch Ltd, Hare Row, London E2 9BY Tel: 071 729 3606
   Wilstow Ltd. (suppliers of Maggiolina tents & Roof Boxes). Tel: 081 871
   5184/5/6
Afri-Quip Ltd. Tel: (0799) 513755
Ropes
H. & T. Marlow Ltd, South Road, Hailsham, Sussex BN27 3JS
Security conversion
Overland Ltd, Link Road, West Wilts Trading Estate, Westbury, Wilts
   BA13 4JB. Tel: (0373) 858272
Shipping agents There are numerous agents – see Yellow Pages. If in
difficulty try:
J.R. & C. Davies, Maritime House, 18 Shore Road, Warsash, Southampton
   SO3 6GQ
Spare-wheel holders
Pivlock Bullivant Engineering, 1 Station Road, Kiveton Park, Nr Sheffield
   S31 8QP
Specialist Vehicles/Importers
Land Leisure UK, Leisure House, Poplar Tree Lane, Rode Common,
   Trowbridge, Wilts BA14 9NB (0373) 831200
   Pinzgauer/Expedition vehicles
Overland Ltd., Link Road, West Wilts Trading Estate, Westbury, Wilts
   BA13 4JB Tel: (0373) 858272
K&J Slavin (Quest) Ltd., Cow Pasture Farm, Louth Road, Hainton,
   Lincolnshire. Tel: (0507) 313401
Suspension
Warwick Banks Handling, West Farm, Witham-on-the-Hill, Bourne, Lincs
   PE 10 OJN
Towing brackets and other accessories
Dixon-Bates, Unit 45, First Avenue, Deeside Industrial Park, Deeside,
   Clwyd CHS 2LG
C P. Witter, 18 Canalside, Chester CH1 3LL
Trailers (DIY)
Indespension, Belmont Road, Bolton BL1 7AQ
Travel Information
The Expedition Advisory Centre, Royal Geographical Society, 1
   Kensington Gore, London SW7 2AR Tel: 071 581 2057
Pieter and Ida Kersten, 79 Palm Straasa, Amsterdam, Holland (A useful
   contact for vehicle preparation/travel in the Sahara.)
The Iceland Centre, 3 Deynecourt, Harrow Park, Harrow on the Hill HA1
   3JE
Winches
Superwinch Ltd, Abbey Rise, Whitchurch Road, Tavistock, Devon PL19
   9DR
Ryders International (Warn Winches), 215 Knowsley Road, Bootle,
   Liverpool L20 4NW Tel: 051 922 7585

Recommended Reading

Available from the LRO Bookshop

A Collector's Guide: The Land Rover 1948-1984, J. Taylor *Driving Techniques,* produced by Land Rover Ltd
Exploring Green Roads and Lanes of Great Britain, I. Thompson
Four-Wheel Drive and Land Rover, N. Baldwin
Four-Wheel Drive Book, J. Jackson
Illustrated History of Off-Road Vehicles, N. Baldwin
Illustrated Jeep Buyer's Guide, P. Sessier
The Jeep, J.G. Jeudy and M. Taraine
Jeep: Mechanical Mule to Peoples' Plaything, H. Rasmussen
Jeep: The 50 Year History, R. Ackerson
Land Rover: the unbeatable 4x4, J. and K. Slavin and G. Mackie
The Landrover: workhorse of the world, G. Robson
Land Rover Series 1,2 & 3: Guide to Purchase and Self Restoration, Lindsay Porter, Haynes
The Off Road and Four-wheel drive Handbook, N. Fryatt
Off Road Guide: Off Roading in Scotland and Europe, C. and P. Berner
Off Road High Performance Handbook, M. Bargo
The Range Rover, J. Taylor
Range Rover Gold Portfolio 1970-1988, published by Brooklands
The Range Rover - Land Rover, G. Robson
Working in the Wild, Land Rover's new manual for Africa

Land Rover Service Publications are available and include workshop manuals, parts catalogues, owner's manuals and service training literature.

Travel and expedition books

Algeria and the Sahara, Valerie and Jon Stevens, Constable, London, 1977.
Exploring Nature in North Africa, Julian Cremona & Robert Chote, Ashford, Southampton, 1989.
Exploring Nature in the Wilds of Europe, Julian Cremona & Robert Chote, Ashford, Southampton, 1988.
A Guide to Land Rover Expeditions, produced and published by Land Rover, Solihull.
Iceland - a handbook for expeditions, Tony Escritt, Iceland Expedition Centre Ltd, London, 1986.
Overland, P. Fraenkel, David and Charles, Newton Abbot, 1975.

The *Rough Guide* series, published by RKP, may be found useful for general guides. Countries include Tunisia, Morocco, Turkey, Scandinavia, France, Spain, Portugal and Greece.

Sahara Handbook, Simon & Jan Glen, Lascelles, 1987.

Through Africa - the Overlanders' Guide, Bob Swain & Paula Snyder, Bradt

The Traveller's Handbook, Ingrid Cranfield, in association with Richard Harrington, Heinemann, London and WEXAS International Ltd, London, 1982. (Incorporates *The Independent Traveller's Handbook* and has contributions from a very wide range of people and topics, with some detailed sections on vehicles, maintenance and driving).

The Tropical Traveller, John Hatt, Pan, London, 1982.

Quick Guide
to Techniques

Summary of descending slopes
- get out and walk it first
- wear safety belts
- select low range
- check first gear is engaged
- pull away - feet off all pedals
- thumbs out of steering wheel spokes
- pick a straight line down

Summary of ascending slopes
- walk right to the top to check the ascent and beyond
- wear seat belts
- select low range
- select suitable gear e.g. second or third
- go up straight

Summary of defaulting on the ascent
- put both feet on the pedal, clutch and brake
- do not use the handbrakes
- quickly select reverse (check you are in low range)
- if engine is running take both feet off clutch and brake pedals together
- If engine is not running: simultaneously with the feet coming off the pedals, turn the ignition key to rotate the engine
- do not brake, use engine braking only
- maintain a straight descent

Summary of traversing side slopes
- avoid driving across a slope whenever possible
  If you have to:
- keep your speed low
- check ground ahead for bumps and dips
- remove any load on top of the vehicle
- eject passengers - if not possible then move them to the high side

Summary of driving rough tracks
- engage FWD on very rough ground and hills
- watch ground clearance, especially beneath diffs.
- drive wheel *over* rocks if necessary
- keep your speed down

Summary of crossing ditches
- slow down
- select low gear
- cross at a 45-degree angle
- one wheel in the ditch at a time

Summary of driving gullies
- walk it first
- select low range
- let passenger direct
- proceed very slowly, following passenger directions only
- keep steering straight

Summary of soft ground driving
- get out and look
- try to gauge depth and slope
- select highest gear, low range, that will pull vehicle through
- try side-to-side steering and blipping of throttle if wheels slip. If forward motion ceases, throttle off, get out and look. Try reverse gear, low range, overdrive engaged if fitted, then high range with FWD/diff. lock if fitted

Summary of wading
- gauge depth and decide suitable route
- check opposite bank for a good exit
- fit wading plug (if any) and check all other waterproofing measures
- select first gear, low range (second if surface soft)
- drive slowly into water, do not stop; maintain a steady, slow speed to obtain a bow wave
- when across, remove wading plug (if any)
- check brakes

Index

217

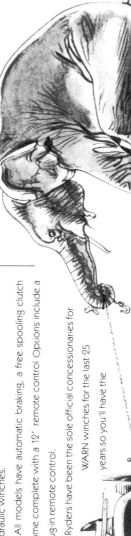

HARTWELL plc

SPECIALISTS ACROSS THE COUNTRY

PLEASE CONTACT:-

Hartwell	Oxford	Telephone	0865 244833
Hartwell	Banbury	Telephone	0295 251551
Hartwell	Wellingborough	Telephone	0933 225506
Hartwell	St Helens	Telephone	0744 26622
Bristol Motor Company		Telephone	0272 266491

NOTES